A 3-in-1 Reference Guide for New and Aspiring Children's Book Authors

Bre'Anna Washington Weatherford

BeeThee.LLC

The Creative Composition Guide to Self-Publishing and Marketing Children's Books
Copyright © 2024 by BeeThee.LLC
Published by BeeThee.LLC BeeTheeART.com
ISBN: 979-8-9887731-7-7

In this book, we share our opinions on best practices that we have researched and used as courses of action to apply toward the objective of this guide. However, we do not guarantee the results of taking any action based on the information provided in this book. The opinions and beliefs in this book are based on information available at the time of writing. This book is intended for personal and educational use only. Our product should not be used as a substitute for financial, legal, or marketing advice. The information in this book is provided "as is" without warranty of any kind, either express or implied. All pricing information is at the time of publication and is subject to vary.

The author and publisher of this book do not accept any liability or responsibility for any loss or damage incurred by individuals or entities in connection with the purchase, download, access, or use of the product. This includes but is not limited to damages for loss of profits and any loss or damage caused by technologically harmful material, whether directly or indirectly caused or alleged to be caused by the information in this book.

All rights reserved. No part of this publication may be reproduced, distributed, or transmitted in any form or by any means, including photocopying, recording, or other electronic or mechanical methods, without the prior written permission of the publisher, except in the case of brief quotations embodied in critical reviews and specific other noncommercial uses.
For permission requests, please contact:
BeeThee.LLC Email: bre@beetheeart.com

LEGO® is a registered trademark of The LEGO Group.

The handwritten font presented in this book was created in Calligraphr.

Printed in the United States of America

To the authors, educators, librarians, and families building communal legacies of literacy and a love for lifelong learning.

To my divine other whole, my light, my husband, my everything: Jeffery. You inspire me in all you do. Thank you for standing as a beacon of unconditional love and support in the truest, purest, and most fortified form.

CONTENTS

Preface..ix

Acknowledgments................................xii

Introduction..xv
    Dear Change-Maker

Chapter 0:..1
    Notes on Nurturing a CREATOR's MINDSET

Chapter 1:..11
    Notes for Writing, Revising, and Researching

Chapter 2:..33
    Notes on Protecting Your Work

Chapter 3:..41
    Notes Before You Hire an Illustrator

Chapter 4:..69
    Notes on Building Your Brand and Online Presence

Chapter 5:..85
    Notes on Hiring and Working with Your Illustrator

Chapter 6:..102
    Notes on Crowdfunding

Chapter 7:..115
    Notes on Distribution and Formatting

Chapter 8:..130
    Notes for Developing a Strong Launch Plan

Chapter 9:..143
  Notes for Marketing Your Book
Glossary..166
Resources & Further Learning...............170
Bibliography..172
About the Author..175

PREFACE

Throughout this guide, I frequently use the term CREATOR in place of author and illustrator to emphasize the breadth of children's book development. The best children's books are made with the support of a team; However, the reality is many of us, in the beginning stages will wear all of the hats, and as budding independent publishers, that may be the case for a while, which is okay. Whether due to finances or timing, you feel like you don't know enough or you think you know it all, even if you're doing this just to say you can. I encourage you to intimately study the information presented in this book and beyond. You want to create a book that you will love and be proud of.

Working closely and effectively with a specialized team will benefit the longevity and expansion of your publishing career, support the overall quality of your children's books, and give you permission to explore more of what you love and are already great at. When you choose to create for children, you become more than an author or illustrator alone; you are part of a greater community committed to a lifetime love of literacy and advocating for the well-being of children. You are a creative reflection of education and art, transforming our relationships through reading. I wrote the Children's Book CREATOR Manifesto as an affirmation of mutual purpose along your journey and a loving reminder that we create better together!

The Children's Book CREATOR MANIFESTO

I am a creator
Part of a benevolent community of fellow dream-makers.
I am a visionary
Dedicated to the advancement of my community.
I commit to working ethically and collectively
To uplift and enrich our families
By embracing the expanse of my creativity.
I trust my ability to inspire positive change
Through my thoughts, my words, my actions and my art.
I am a creator.
I create from my heart.

Est. 2024 beethee.llc

If you want to go fast, go alone. If you want to go far, go together.
                              -African Proverb

ACKNOWLEDGMENTS

Thank you, Mom, Donna, for taking the time to read with me early and often and encouraging me to surround myself with people who want the best for me and themselves. Thank you for "putting me out there" in every play, concert easter speech, and liturgical contest.

Thank you to my mother-in-love, Carole, for your tough love, patient guidance, exemplary dedication to preserving our histories, and delivering the truth through children's literature.

Thank you, Rubie Britt-Height and my Mint Museum Grier Heights family, thank you for encouraging me to remain the artist I was born to be. For introducing me to artists and leaders who look like me and for your continuous support as I continue your work to inspire the next generation.

Thank you as well to the following people:

My Soul Sister Alora Pope De Calero
My Holistic Wellness Team Aura Luv, Jessie, and Delilah
My Business Coach Jalynn Jones and The Black Pretty and Paid University Team

Influential Author and Book Coach, Dr. Jasmine Womack and The EMPACT Group
My Writing Partner Dr. Uchenna E. Miles
Author Felicia K. Brookins
Editor and co-designer Caroline Smith
Brick 22 Productions

Supporting Authors and Illustrators:

Kim C. Lee
Mike and Barbara Gammage
Nia Yaa Nebehet
Naomi V. Dunsen-White
The Mariam Poppins Team
Dedrick and Haelee Moone
Nia Obotette
Travis Thompson
Wolly V.
Tiffany Semmons
Ife, Mujasi, and Nyame Fatiu
Osunfemi Wanbi Njeri
Abigale Roscoe
KP Carter
Kimberly Davis Peters
Tiffany Obeng
Ashley and Thao (Galaxy Gals Studios)

Dear Change-Maker,

Congratulations and thank you! You are well on your way to self-publishing your first or next great children's book! Even if this is not your first, I celebrate you for being open to a broader perspective in publishing and marketing, and I am grateful you chose my *Creative Composition Guide* as your self-publishing companion!

I am Bre'Anna Washington-Weatherford, lovingly known as "Bee." I am an illustrator, educator, spoken word artist, and creativity coach. I have served as an art educator and mentor for over seven years in my community, and I have been helping make authors' dreams come true through illustration and publishing for nearly five years. I am the co-coordinator, lead educator, and former student of The Grier Heights Youth Arts Program. This after-school program has been a beacon for arts education, self-expression, and community pride for children and their families for nineteen years and counting. A program for which I am forever grateful, as it continued to nourish my love and talent for art outside of school and gave me the freedom and opportunity to expand into the person I am today.

In July 2019, following my internship at The Smithsonian Museum of African Art, I was accepted for an interim position at The Mint Museum to support the Learning and Engagement Department with a major illustration exhibition - "the most extensive look at the art of book illustration" they have ever done. During that exhibition, my world became much smaller and simultaneously much more expansive. There, I met multi-award-winning illustrator Vanessa Brantley Newton, who encouraged me to lean deeper into illustration as a career with wisdom toward community and as a primary example of what is possible.

When I initially embarked on my illustration career, like many new illustrators and authors, I thought I'd be exclusively drawing pictures for a living. "I'll draw pictures, and they'll love them, and they'll pay me. Easy." This was my life for about three months, as the first illustrated title I worked on was a collaborative crowdfunding project that served as my initiation of the ins and outs, ups and downs of self-publishing and marketing children's books. Supporting authors throughout the publishing and marketing process felt natural and I enjoy seeing the beautiful evolution of what was once a dream transform into a physical manifestation. A book is one of the greatest treasures you can gift someone, one of those gifts that never stop giving, and while it may be foolish to think we could read every book that we pack on our library shelves, you can write that one book that can change a child's life, only if they get the chance to see it.

Many authors with a genuine passion for sharing meaningful experiences with children struggle to jumpstart and maintain their children's book careers by feeling like they have to navigate it alone, by choice, or by force, leading them to take shortcuts, rush the process, or stop.

"I've written my children's book...Now What?"

The "...now what?" is what *The Creative Composition Guide to Self-Publishing and Marketing Children's Books* aims to support you through. While many channels and platforms are available to teach authors how to write, publish, and market children's books, *The Creative Composition Guide* provides concise, structured "Notes" from behind the scenes utilizing my experiences and research, as well as anecdotes from my community of bestselling authors, illustrators, editors, coaches, and mentors.

For nearly five years, I have had the pleasure of floating between worlds supporting authors, illustrators, and designers in both traditional and self-publishing, which has helped cultivate this multidimensional perspective and approach to publishing and marketing children's books.

The Creative Composition Guide is not a writer's manual. Use this as your curated reference guide complete with running lists, market research, and your bright book ideas! I saved space for you, so unless you're checking this out from your local library, feel encouraged to write in this book, and any time you see, TAKE ACTION, take a breath, and do just that. While I recommend you read in order, you can reference the 'Notes' of your choice, read the entire chapter, and then apply what you've learned.

I appreciate the authors who have entrusted me with translating their ideas into illustrations to help them launch their children's books. Furthermore, I am grateful for the countless hours spent in creative consultation with my team that helped me write this 3-in-1 guidebook. Like any significant project, a lot of planning, writing, drawing, community engagement, important conversations, mistakes, sacrifices, and outright failures were made during the creation of this book. These experiences have humbled me and taught me to lean into the love and guidance of my support system; in addition to my family, I am grateful to be able to invest in regular therapy and enlist the support of trusted business coaches. They have helped me stay open to being inspired and intentional about investing more in what sparks joy and have made room for greater clarity in purpose and truth in service to see my ideal vision of success. It's my biggest wish that *The Creative Composition Guide to Self-Publishing and Marketing Children's Books* will do the same for you.

In the words of the great mother, Maya Angelou:

Success is liking yourself, liking what you do, and liking how you do it.

Creating for children is one of the most rewarding things I do. I wrote this book as a personal affirmation for myself and as encouragement for you along your journey. Enjoy the process; your work leads legacies and leaves a lasting and loving impact on children and their families.

This guide is for creators passionate about healthy childhood development and providing sensational literary experiences for their community.

If you are reading this, you are my kind of creator; thank you again for your love and dedication to being a change-maker and advocate for lifelong learning. Thank you for taking the serious next steps in your journey as a self-published children's book author and choosing this guide to support you through to your success!

If there's anything that resonates with you or anything you disagree with, don't hesitate to reach out to me or leave a review on your favorite platform and tag me.

I appreciate all feedback, and I look forward to seeing you shine!

Remember to take your time, trust yourself, your creativity, and your ability to act toward fulfilling your dreams.

Lovingly,
Bre'Anna Washington-Weatherford
Author-Illustrator, Educator, Creativity Coach
BeeTheeART.com

CHAPTER 0: NOTES ON NURTURING A CREATOR'S MINDSET

On Being a C.R.E.A.T.O.R.

While writing your children's book may have come as second nature, your goal now is to elevate into an independent publisher and ensure your work finds its way into the hearts and homes of eager young readers and their families. Being a creator means embracing each opportunity to build intentional, impactful relationships. Let your children's book be a natural extension of the work you are already doing and are passionate about. Stay curious,

> *Self-avoidance is futile. Believe in your unique gifts and know they will impact the world. Turn inward and do your own self-inquiry. Be your own student.*
>
> -Latham Thomas, Author and doula

embrace your strengths, and identify how you can actively incorporate your natural greatness into your children's book journey.

Many great philosophers, authors, artists, doctors, and scientists across time have spoken and still speak on the power and importance of developing healthy habits and a healthy mindset. How you think, feel, speak about, and see yourself and your endeavors will reflect in every aspect of your life including your children's book journey. I challenge you to believe in your ability to inspire, educate, and enrich families through your children's books. When you understand the power of your mindset, you will know that you already have everything you need to become the children's book creator you aspire to be.

CLARIFY YOUR "*WHY*"

Passion is organic; when you sit down to do something you love, why isn't the first question you ask yourself, you just do it. Between accessing your tools and support, knowing your timeline, and establishing your budget you'll likely wonder, "How did I get myself into this?", "Is it all necessary?" "Is it really worth it to finish?" Knowing and reminding yourself why you started in the first place and visualizing how it will feel for you and the families who need your book to have it, grow from it, and use it to change the world. That's a powerful push! If you let it, your why can be contagious, connecting you to the communities, experiences, and overall expansion of your children's book career. Remember, in all the work you do you have the potential to make a child feel seen, safe, and capable of being themselves and accomplishing their dreams, you also have the potential to bring families and communities closer together. Now, I can tell you this all day, but it takes time and continual work for you to identify what you are genuinely seeking to accomplish through your children's book career. Maybe you want to encourage families to take better care of their health, highlight an underrepresented culture, or spend more time embracing their imagination; and what else is that connected to? Your *why* will change and mature as you do, but approaching each step of your journey with examined intent and passion will help you see, plan, and make informed decisions on your path to success.

You may already be clear on your why. Still, whether you're entirely sure or not quite there yet, I encourage you to engage in regular meditative or enlightening practices as a physical reminder of your light, openness, and capability to overcome. This may be sitting quietly, but it doesn't have to be; your meditative or enlightening practice can be anything you choose that allows you to feel restful or joyous. For some, it could be embroidery; for others, it could be journaling, roller skating, or scheduling time to recharge and unplug fully. My husband and I recently took up float therapy to improve our meditative practices. Whatever it is, take the time to do it daily or a few times a week to help you stay grounded and connected to your *why*, and at times when your why doesn't feel like enough, I encourage you to give yourself permission and grace to pause, reset, and lean into what you love.

RESEARCH AND PLAN

This is your sustenance. Creating a children's book involves a unique consideration - not only are you considering your young  readers and what resonates with them, but you're also considering the adults who love and care for them; they will ultimately be your target market and the ones investing in your book. Your pursuit of research becomes fuel for the journey to connect with both these audiences effectively. Schedule time in the spaces where your audience is, what they are looking for, picking up, and purchasing. These unique perspectives can help you tailor your book to resonate with both kids and their guardians. Research is a continuous and ever-evolving process. It's also your ticket to saving valuable time and resources to acquire your dream team. Staying updated with industry trends, seeking answers in your local social media group, conducting dedicated research, and having a thoughtful plan will help you stay accountable, excited for the future, and establish a budget beforehand to prepare you to fund the costs of publishing and investing in your professional development as an author. Investing in conferences, workshops, festivals, and mentorship will help you learn with and from all kinds of book buddies from other authors and illustrators to parents, educators, librarians, and publishers. Stay curious and stay connected.

EMBRACE GROWTH

Building a career in children's books will take time, resources, a team, and a series of plans and strategies and anyone looking to opt for the fast and free package, prepare to be sorely disappointed. Embrace the time it takes to grow and learn every step of the way and maximize the relationships you build to create the outcomes you desire. This journey will stretch you, so I encourage you to take intentional time reflect, and reframe your challenges as growth opportunities. Like all things, your journey as a children's book creator will change with the seasons, but each one brings opportunities for growth and expansion.

ARTICULATE YOUR GOALS & ACQUIRE YOUR TEAM

When you have a foundational understanding of the mindset and resources it will take to transform from a children's book writer to a published author, it's time to implement that understanding. Define your objectives and establish measurable goals for your children's book project. This guide was written to take you to school, this step involves more than just setting vague intentions. So, write down those S.M.A.R.T. goals for your children's book project.

S - Specific

M - Measurable.

A - Actionable

R - Relevant

T - Timely

This practice will help you develop and articulate your goals for creation, collaboration, sales, reviews, and re-engagement. Write down your goals in detail and break out your K.W.L.D. chart! Get clear on what you:

K – know and love, what you

W – want to learn, and what you've

L – learned and prefer to...

D – delegate to your team.

TEST AND TAILOR

One of the best things I could have done for this project was to share my ideas with the experts in my circle and future children's book creators who would benefit from this resource. That's where many new authors fall short, whether it's afraid of failure, judgment, or—my favorite—the fear of success; you'll have to do some practice runs with your audience if you want to craft a book that resonates and sells, not just to your family and friends but to the communities of educators, librarians, museum professionals and families who will love and benefit from your book for generations.

Your creative work should align seamlessly with your *why* on and off social platforms. It should be easy to find you, what you do, and how you use what you do to help others. As a children's book author, your content does not have to always be about children's books, but it would behoove you to keep it family-friendly and in context. Your content should captivate their attention and add genuine value to their lives. It could be in the form of laughter, education, or aesthetic appeal, but when you are connected to your why, it becomes easier to see how every step in your journey can also be connected.

ORGANIZE AND STRATEGIZE

Your tailored content lets you discover what works, what won't, and what needs work. The success of your journey from a children's book writer to a published author depends significantly on your ability to organize and execute thoughtful strategies. These strategies guide you toward your objectives while ensuring that all your actions and decisions remain harmoniously aligned with your larger *why*. This means staying consistent and organized and using *The Creative Composition Guide* to support you in creating an outline for your pre-publishing, publishing, marketing, and sales goals while remaining flexible enough to adapt to the changing market.

REFLECT, REFINE, AND RETAIN

Take time to reflect on your journey often and celebrate yourself, even your seemingly small wins, for staying committed to becoming a published children's book author. As feedback comes in, as you gain experience, and as market conditions evolve, be open to adapting to continue to meet your goals. The key to staying relevant and ensuring your work remains practical and appealing to your readers is to be yourself and listen to those who you have taken time to invest in and those who have taken time to invest in you. You are creating a community and culture around your book; think about how you want to continue and maintain that community. Adopting a CREATOR mindset of constant improvement fuels your journey toward becoming a successful children's book author and independent publisher. Children deserve stories that inspire, grow with them, and make them feel seen and heard. Now that we've set the stage with the right mindset let's dive into crafting your children's book with confidence, purpose, and clarity. Enjoy the process and create a book your inner child will love!

There was no way I could have finished this book if I had included every thought and resource I could think of, so I have compiled a page with a host of resources for your reference including a self-publishing checklist, ways to connect with your audience, and ideas for you to build from that will help you eliminate friction at every level of your journey. This is an expanding VIP C.R.E.A.T.O.R. Library that I update regularly. You can access this page by following the QR code below to create a free account at BeeTheeART.com, there you can view and print your resources at will.

CHAPTER 1: NOTES FOR WRITING, REVISING, AND RESEARCHING

KEEP YOUR SPECIFIC READER IN MIND

Before we get started...Take a few deep breaths...

And visualize...

The families that will be reading your book...

The children that will be reading your book...

Where are they?

What do they need most?

How can your book support them?

Keeping your specific reader in mind is important when writing, revising, and researching your publishing journey. Putting your ideal reader at the forefront of your mind will train your eye to see what will speak to them. This will set you apart in creating a book that appeals to your readers and keeps them engaged. See the story from their perspective and consider what would resonate most with them.

You may have finished or written a significant portion of your children's book but consider a few key details to ensure you're publishing a book that will connect with the families that will love it the most before you commit to your current manuscript.

1. **What is your ideal reader's age range and interests?** What kind of story are you creating? How are your characters and themes relevant to the children and families who will read your books? How old is your audience? What grade are they in?

2. **Enlist feedback from early readers.** This will help you to see what's working and what needs improvement and give you a significant edge in marketing. Keep in touch with your early readers; they will transform into your Launch Team.

3. **Hire an editor.** Someone knowledgeable in children's book publishing. No matter how short your book is or how great you think your writing is, you will benefit from having another

professional edit your work. Ask any self-publishing professional; skipping the editing process is one of most new authors' biggest mistakes in writing for children. That, and opting for poor illustrations.

> *Research is formalized curiosity. It's poking and prying with a purpose.*
>
> -Zora Neale Hurston, American author, and anthropologist

Children's books have a wide and varied readership from newborns to eighteen-year-olds. However, when it comes to marketing your book, your primary focus should be reaching and engaging with the caregivers of these children. It's crucial to clearly understand whom your book is addressing and whom your marketing efforts are targeting so you can speak directly to them. This approach is instrumental in creating a book families will love and relate to and will help to build a solid and devoted fanbase for your work.

Children deserve high-quality, relevant books that allow them to be seen and heard. Loved ones are always looking for engaging and meaningful stories whose lessons will grow with them, and if you can connect with them on a deeper level, they'll eagerly purchase your books, share them with others, and come back for more. I'm still collecting books and treasuries of stories I loved in childhood for myself and my family. Give your audience something that they can hold on to.

WHAT IS A HIGH-QUALITY CHILDREN'S BOOK?

You're not going to produce a high-quality children's book for free, but that doesn't mean you have to invest your life savings into it. A high-quality children's book is thoughtfully curated with children and their families in mind and is produced by a team of dedicated creators focused on enriching the lives of their readers. A high-quality children's book is kid-tested, approved, beautifully illustrated, relevant, and engaging. We have the responsibility to provide these experiences for children. Just because self-publishing content for children is hot right now doesn't mean you should. Especially if you are unwilling to do your research, you want to start a quick side hustle, or you're not genuinely interested in making children feel seen, heard, and safe. We don't just buy any book for the children we love; we buy the best.

STAY CURIOUS

In addition to writing and revising, you will research continuously with your audience in mind. Look for books that are similar to yours and see what readers are saying about them. This can help you identify what works and doesn't in your genre. With so many different types of children's books available, it can be challenging to determine which one you are creating. If you need more clarification, I have included a chart showing various types of children's books with examples. For more information, check out Fig. 1, "Children's Book Type" Chart, there will be some exceptions and nuances to this if you're working in verse, publishing a treasury or anthology of stories.

Here are some pro tips to keep in mind during your research:

- Pay attention to positive and negative reviews to understand what readers like and dislike about the books in your genre.

- Spend time studying book anatomy in local bookstores and libraries.

- Search hashtags and attend book fairs and conferences where authors and readers are to learn about new books and trends.

- Dare to read outside your genre. Reading widely across different genres can help you better understand storytelling techniques and audience expectations.

- Find and engage with a writers' community based on your book theme and genre.

STAY ORGANIZED

Keep a digital running document alongside your *Creative Composition Guide* with your book title, description, genre, keywords, and categories; this will all serve as your **metadata**. From identifying your target market through advertising your metadata is vital in helping book buyers and search engines categorize and distribute your book effectively, enhancing its visibility and overall accessibility in the marketplace. We'll discuss this in Chapter 9: Notes on Marketing your book, but as I've learned in my years of education, it's important to begin with the end in mind. You can organize your metadata in an Excel document, phone notes, or a platform that supports a more detailed workflow like Notion, Slack,

Milanote, Freeform, or Trello. As you continue your book study, stay mindful of your audience and the nuances of your specific book. While I have listed a few books for your reference, one of the best ways to study books is at your local library or bookstore, where everything is organized and people are there to support you, additionally, you can use their companion Libby app to search and study a variety of eBooks.

CHILDREN'S BOOK TYPE CHART

TYPE	AVERAGE WORD COUNT	EXAMPLES
BOARD BOOKS	0-100	*Me and The Family Tree* Carole Boston Weatherford Illustrated by Ashleigh Corrin *Bright Brown Baby* Series Andrea Davis Pinkney Illustrated by Brian Pinkney
EARLY READERS EARLY CHAPTERS	100-500 500-1,200	*Ty's Travels* Series Kelly Starling Lyons Illustrated by Nina Mata *Yasmine* Series Saadia Faruqi illustrated by Hatem Aly

FICTION PICTURE BOOKS (REALISTIC) (HISTORICAL)	500 - 1,000 1,200 - 1,500	*Milo Imagines The World* Matt de la Peña and Christian Robinson *That Flag* Tameka Fryer Brown and Nikkolas Smith
NON-FICTION PICTURE BOOKS	1000 - 2,500	*The Ashe Brothers: How Arthur and Johnnie Changed Tennis Forever* Judy Allen Dodson *Hidden Figures: The True Story of Four Black Women and the Space Race.* Margot Lee Shetterly Illustrated by Laura Freeman
GRAPHIC NOVELS	20,000 - 50,000	*Like Lava in My Veins* Derrick Barnes Illustrated by Shawn Martinbrough *Black Sands Comic Series* Black Sands Entertainment

MG CHAPTER BOOKS	25,000 - 45,000	*Onyeka and The Academy of the Sun* Tola Okogwu *One Crazy Summer* Rita Williams-Garcia
MIDDLE GRADES	20,000 - 45,000	*Root Magic* Eyden Royce *Kin: Rooted in Hope* Carole Boston Weatherford and Jeffery Boston Weatherford
YOUNG ADULT	60,000 - 90,000	*Legacy of the Orisha Series* Tomi Adeyemi *Genesis Begins Again* Alicia D. Williams

TAKE ACTION 1.1

What is the title of your book?

What type of children's book are you creating?

What is your book about?

Who is your ideal reader? How old are they, and what are they interested in? What do they feel? How do they interact with their environment?

Why would caregivers want to share your book with the children they love?

The 5-10 people whose opinions I trust are... (*Think of people who can benefit from your book and those who could support you in developing your book.*)

TAKE ACTION 1.2

What are the top 5-10 children's books in your genre and topic? What's working, and where do you see improvements could be made? You can use the example below to start your list of top books. Take note of the keywords and categories_you will need these when you are ready to publish. Publisher Rocket is a great tool to help you search strong keywords and categories in your children's book topic.

Book:

Rating:

Reviews:

Categories:

Keywords:

Book:

Rating:

Reviews:

Categories:

Keywords:

Book:

Rating:

Reviews:

Categories:

Keywords:

Book:

Rating:

Reviews:

Categories:

Keywords:

Book:

Rating:

Reviews:

Categories:

Keywords:

TAKE ACTION 1.3

What makes your book unique for your ideal reader?

Based on the reviews, evaluate the strengths and weaknesses of each book.

How does your book address or improve upon these strengths and weaknesses?

Are there any gaps or opportunities in the market that your book can fill?

SECURE AN EDITOR

It doesn't matter how short your manuscript is or how great of a writer you are. You're going to need a good editor on your team. When securing the right editor for your  children's book, consider how your book reads; editors can specialize in various literary styles, including but not limited to rhyme and verse, young adult stories, non-fiction, and informational text for children. Reedsy.com is a great platform to find and hire an expert editor. A quick search within your favorite author groups will give you a clear and vetted list of editors and dozens of authors who have asked and answered some of the same questions you have before. Look for editors that people have frequently recommended and browse their websites. Many professional editors will provide you with a free review and sample edit before you decide if the two of you would be a good working fit. Some things cannot be solely understood through text, with any collaboration, it's important to have a clear way to communicate with your service providers, before you hire them and throughout the agreed service timeline.

Joining a critique group will also help provide that brutally honest feedback that no one wants, but every creator needs to hear. If you're genuinely working to improve your writing and build your confidence as an author, a great way to do that is through a dedicated community. I met with a client who expressed their fear of critiques on their work, so if you're feeling something similar remember critique groups are not a judgment on your person or character. A critique group is an intentional space and opportunity for your work to improve. You don't have to take everything you hear. You'll find what feels right for you and your readers: the children and families who will benefit most from your book.

I have subscribed to my fair share of children's book communities, which has helped me receive direct feedback and connect with fellow book creators at all levels of creation. Alternatively, if you know an English teacher, you could offer to meet them for coffee and invite them to be one of your beta readers. Some developmental editing can be achieved with a few dependable beta readers.

EDITORS

NAME	CONTACT	EST. COST	NOTES/ DELIVERABLES
NAOMI V.	naomibooks.com		
EDITOR CAROLINE	editorcaroline.com		
ABDUL ALI	abdulali.net		

TAKE ACTION 1.4

Share with some early readers. It's above you now, so take a break; you've done it! You've written your children's book or at least have a solid draft ready. While waiting for your editor, take some time to test-run your book. You may, and I strongly encourage you to copy-write your manuscript first. You can use Chapter 4, "Notes on Protecting Your Work," for guidance on securing your copywrite, ISBN, and Library of Congress Number. You could share a protected file with honest friends, host a read-aloud, or share your story with your critique group. I know it's scary, and this next part may be harsh, but it's not about you anymore. Our obligation, as creatives, is to share our gifts and talents with the world. I, too, was afraid of sharing this book with you, but we must trust that no one can do what you do like you do it! That's been my mantra for this task:

> *No one can do what I do like I do!*

That last part is vital; it is an affirmation for when you feel self-doubt creep in. A serious independent publisher will put their book ideas into the world *before* they are ready. This will help you learn, engage, build with your ideal reader, and create a book they will love, buy, and share! Best-selling author Kim C. Lee emphasizes that "self-publishing children's books is a long-term game that requires continuous promotion." I would add PRE-promotion and "just because it's released doesn't mean promotion should stop." Therefore, finding creative ways to market your book continuously is important.

TAKE ACTION 1.5

Write a list of at least seven affirmations to keep close to your heart along your author journey. Remind yourself of your greatness and potential daily. This practice and daily gratitude will significantly shift your focus toward your inevitable success. Start from the bottom and build up.

7. **I** trust

6. **I** see

5. **I** speak

4. **I** love

3. **I** know

2. **I** feel

1. **I** am

TAKE ACTION 1.6

Locate your local bookstores and libraries and spend some time among their shelves. Note your discoveries: What books do you love? Are there books similar to yours? What books are people checking out or purchasing the most and how much do they cost on average? Additionally, look at books for sizing, colors, graphics, etc. to get inspiration for your cover or what types of illustrations you would like.

You can find your local bookstores at indiebound.org[1] and bookshop.org[2]

---

[1] https://www.indiebound.org/indie-store-finder
[2] https://bookshop.org/pages/bookstores

TAKE ACTION 1.7

Are any book fairs or related events coming up in the next three to five months? Write them down NOW, then put them on your calendar. While you may only go to some of them, use this list to call in the energy and experiences of your ideal reader. Explore: this will be a helpful tool when building your brand and social sites.

CHAPTER 2: NOTES ON PROTECTING YOUR WORK

THREE KEYS

If you would like to copyright your manuscript before you begin sharing it with others you can do so when you have a final draft, but it's important to note if you copyright your manuscript before your illustrations are complete, you'll need to file and pay for an additional copyright following completion. Your copyright could take up to six months to receive, but it will not prevent you from publishing your book on time. While you do claim copyright over your book the moment you begin writing, to protect your right as a publisher legally, you'll want to file for copyright.[3] You'll also want to obtain an ISBN for

---

[3] Alexa Bigwarfe, "What Every Author Needs to Know about Copyright, ISBN, PCN and LCCN - Write: PUBLISH: Sell," https://writepublishsell.com/, June 28, 2023, https://writepublishsell.com/isbn-lccn-copyright/.

each book format. While your Library of Congress Number (LCCN) is optional, who doesn't want their book cataloged in the most extensive library in the world? This number is also necessary for legal purposes; when someone wants permission to use your work, note that you cannot acquire your LCCN after you publish your book. Additional protections include filling trademarks for systems related to your book. This is worth looking into especially if you plan on publishing a series and using your characters in product designs.

To obtain an ISBN, complete the application and visit the <u>Bowker Identifier Services website</u>. They are starting at $195.00 for one and $295.00 for 10. Bowker is the only US-recognized ISBN Service. If you purchase ISBNs from anyone else, they are considered the publisher, not you, and you limit your ability to determine where you would like to sell your book. You can get free ISBNs from both Ingram Spark and Amazon; however, if you would like to publish your book on another platform, you will not be able to transfer the same ISBN to the additional platform and will need to apply for a separate one. **To apply for an LCCN,** visit the Library of Congress website. Once on the site, go to the <u>Services</u> category in the Menu, find Publishing, and select "PrePub Book Link" and "Author Portal" to apply. You must provide information about the book, yourself as the author, and the ISBN. Once you've submitted your application, you'll receive a confirmation with the case number for your copyright application and your book's Library of Congress Control Number (LCCN).

To **apply** for a US Copyright, visit www.copyright.gov website, select the "Registration" tab, choose the "Literary Works" category, and scroll down to select "Register Literary Work" to complete the application. It will cost around $35-85, depending on the work you are registering for.

> **Pro Tip:**
> It's important to note if you are hiring an illustrator, the Work for Hire document should include details about whether the illustrator or author obtains the image copyright.

I am not a tax professional or legal expert, however you should always consider some legal protection over your intellectual property. When purchasing your copyright and ISBN, consider whether you would like to publish under your name, business name, LLC, publishing imprint, or pen name. Regardless of your choice, ensure you present adequate tax information in your back channels to receive and track income appropriately.

For example, if you publish under the pen name Ms. Mystery but your name is Erica Cooper, as long as your tax information routes to Erica Cooper, you can publish under your desired name.

MORE ON YOUR ISBN

An International Standard Book Number (ISBN) is a unique identifier assigned to each published  book and is essential for tracking it in the publishing industry. As an independent publisher, you must purchase your ISBN to claim full ownership and generate income from your book sales. If you outsource your publishing, having your own ISBN will give you an upper hand in negotiating royalty rates. Purchasing a batch of ISBNs is recommended if you plan to publish in multiple formats and if you plan to publish multiple books, as each requires its unique ISBN. Even if you decide to publish a coloring book, you will need an ISBN. Think of it as providing each version its passport to the world. There is no need to purchase barcodes as they can be made for free by your designer or provided upon publishing.

KNOW YOUR OPTIONS

It's common to hear the terms "hybrid," "boutique," or "vanity" publishing used interchangeably, but they are not the same. Depending on the support you require, you may veer from self-publishing. It's critical to be cautious and avoid vanity press companies disguised as publishers. These entities usually send unsolicited emails and messages about how great they think your book is but then ask you to pay them to publish your book. The difference between a legitimate self-publishing service company and a vanity press is you know exactly who you're paying and what you're paying for.

As an independent publisher, you are responsible for vetting, hiring, and building your team, learning your tools, and fine-tuning your systems. With the increasing accessibility of print-on-demand and e-book services like Ingram Spark, Kindle Direct Publishing, and Draft 2 Digital, you can design, upload, print, and ship your books at no upfront cost to you. However, it's important to remember that a high-quality self-published book takes a team effort. Therefore, knowing your self-publishing options and making informed decisions before outsourcing is crucial.

I met an author during an indie-publishing conference who was searching for ways to outsource their workload so they could focus on what they loved; they were surprised when they realized that the rights and royalties to their book only partly belonged to them. They admit this may have been a positive experience had they known fully what they signed up for. However, in their excitement, they missed some essential details. The author's story prompted me to better understand the self-publishing process and the pros and cons of both boutique and hybrid publishing, which are similar, but the key is in knowing who owns the rights to publishing the book. Ownership of your ISBN, LCCN, and Copyright ensures you are the "majority rights owner." The majority owner gets the majority of the royalties because they do a majority of the work and also are responsible for all of the registrations (and the associated cost).

HYBRID VS. BOUTIQUE

In both boutique and hybrid publishing, there is an element of traditional publishing that could be beneficial to new authors who know what they are investing in and understand the royalty split. Hybrid publishing is a popular option for new authors. It combines the advantages of both DIY and outsourcing. It is a "you choose" approach, which means that as an author, you can research and hire the best professionals from your network, such as editors, illustrators, and designers, for the specific services you require. You decide how your book is printed, distributed, and marketed. Additionally, you will purchase your own ISBN and retain full rights and royalties over your book. Boutique publishing is a "publisher's choice" method, meaning they work within their network to publish your book and you are paying for the connections and services the publisher already has. They may also offer marketing advice or courses in addition to their done-for-you services. Some boutique publishers specialize in specific niches like art, emotions, nature, poetry, or local history. You may be required to submit a query to be considered for a boutique publisher. A boutique publisher will charge an upfront fee to publish your book with the possibility of a royalty split if they provide you with an ISBN. Boutique publishers see their authors as partners in the creative process and with the support of various teams within the publishing house they offer tailored and personalized support throughout publishing and marketing.

TAKE ACTION 2.1

You can jot down your essential need-to-know numbers here:

ISBN:

Hardcover:

Softcover:

E-book:

Audio:

Coloring Book:

Other Formats:

Copyright date:

LCCN:

Trademark Information:

CHAPTER 3: NOTES BEFORE YOU HIRE AN ILLUSTRATOR

KNOW YOUR VISION

Now that you've done some initial research to identify and understand your ideal reader, it's time to decide what illustrations will enhance your book. Depending on your readers' genre, age range, and interests, you aim to capture the right illustrations for a holistic experience for your readers. You may have noticed certain illustration styles and themes that aligned well with your story throughout your research. For instance, if your book revolves around a kindergarten spring break trip, a light watercolor look and feel would complement the warm and playful atmosphere of the story. On the other hand, if you're writing a young adult science fiction novel, you may lean towards dark space blues, purples, and black and white interior images to create a more sophisticated and atmospheric tone.

This knowledge will help you streamline hiring when looking through illustrator portfolios. You can quickly identify illustrators whose work aligns with your creative vision by clearly defining the artistic style that resonates with your story. The "Illustration Styles Chart" (Fig. 2) can be a valuable tool to help you determine the preferred look for your illustrations. By using these prompts to research images in similar styles, you can better visualize how the illustrations will complement your story even before diving into artists' portfolios.

ILLUSTRATION STYLES CHART

STYLES	DESCRIPTION
WATERCOLOR	Watercolor is soft and dreamy images with beautiful washes of color. Watercolors can inspire lighter, calmer moods.
PEN AND INK / BLACK AND WHITE STYLES	Pen and ink images provide High-contras, bold lines and intricate shading. These are primarily used in chapter books, comic books, and young adult books.
DIGITAL	Digital art is versatile and can incorporate a variety of styles from vector building and 3D Modeling to digital drawing, painting, and collage. A great digital artist can recreate many traditional art mediums.

COLLAGE	Collage is cut-out images, textures, and patterns to create whimsical, or intricate layered images, paintings, and drawings with a playful, handmade feel.
REALISTIC	Realistic illustrations are more true to life, often using detailed shading and precise proportions. Photography-based books would fit into this style.
CARTOON	Cartoon style images simplify and exaggerate shapes and features to create playful and younger images.
GRAPHIC	Graphic illustrations, provide bold lines, shapes, and colors to create simple, eye-catching images with a modern, minimalist feel. Similar to digital but can be made using traditional methods.

KNOW YOUR BOOK SPECIFICATIONS

Before hiring your illustrator, knowing, and committing to your book specifications is essential, as it helps your illustrator draw to scale to ensure high-quality printing. Learning your book specs includes having an accurate page count and knowing the trim size. Additionally, if you are planning to format your interior layout, you'll need to know your bleed, margins, and the desired formats for publishing your book. This impacts the visual appeal, printing, and sales costs and will help you create a solid outline for reference with your illustrator and book designer, saving you money in the long run.[4]

TRIM SIZE

Trim size refers to the final dimensions of a printed book after it has been cut and bound. It is an important consideration for authors and publishers because it affects the overall look and feel of the book, as well as its production costs and pricing. Choosing the correct trim size for your book can help ensure that it looks professional and

---

[4] https://brookevitale.com/blog/childrens-book-layout#3-set-page-turns , A Template for Children's Book Layout, Pagination & Design Children's Book Template | Children's Book Layout | Story Pacing Last updated on: November 03, 2023 Brooke Vitale, Children's Book Editorial Services.

is cost-effective to produce. We will discuss bleed and margins in later formatting chapters; however, if you hire a professional illustrator, they will know how to scale and export their illustrations to accommodate the bleed based on your trim size and page count. Your designer or someone who knows how to format children's books will also be helpful with making minute adjustments to preserve the book's quality. Here are some common book dimensions to help you get started.

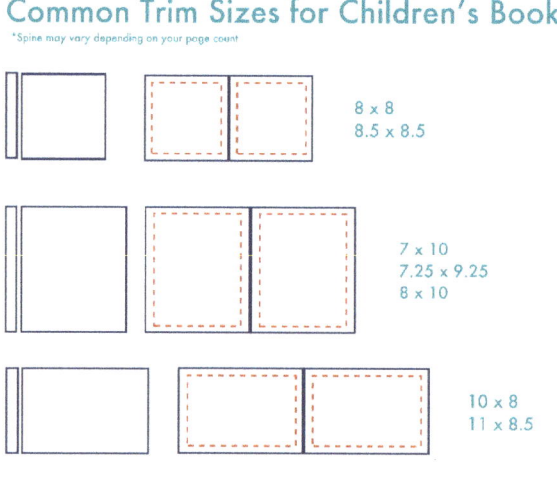

The images above are just a few examples of common children's book sizes. You can access more in your CREATOR Library. If you're working on this venture solo, we'll discuss bleed and margins in

Chapter 7: Notes on Formatting and Preparing Your Book for Print.

CREATE A PICTURE BOOK OUTLINE (DUMMY/STORYBOARD)

You most likely have a firm idea of what you want your book scenes to look like in your head; creating a picture book outline will help you clarify your vision and communicate confidently with your team. Creating a picture book outline is a great practice to organize your thoughts and overall book vision. It will set you apart in hiring, save money, and help you develop a strong foundation for your illustrator to reference. To make great books, you have to study great books, so I urge you to learn some picture book mechanics. Reading a picture book is different from studying because studying a picture book focuses on the anatomy and the book's development. I am in an illustration course where my instructor recommends that we study 100 picture books. I highly recommend doing the same to stay current on what makes a great children's book inside and out. As an independent publisher, it will benefit you and your book sales immensely to know the publishing and marketing standards of the professionals.

Review the books in your genre and age group often and look for these additional design elements when deciding how you want your book to present and what type of illustrations will best support your vision. This is your book anatomy, and these small details can save you and your illustrator time and resources, and that will support your book with a dynamic and professional look and feel.

> You can't use up creativity. The more you use, the more you have.
> -Maya Angelou

BOOK ANATOMY CHART

TERM	DESCRIPTION	ARTIST TOUCH
END PAGES	Decorative patterns or designs that appear at the beginning of a book before the title page, set the tone for the book	Decoration
SPOTS	Palm-sized companion illustrations that stand alone without a background.	Page Turners
HALF PAGE	Useful in providing a direct text-to-image reference.	Visual Context and Reference
SINGLE PAGE	Presented on one side and text on another.	Visual Anchor and Emotional Impact
DOUBLE PAGE (FULL SPREAD)	Detailed illustrations typically depict major scenes or large groups or spanning across two pages.	Immersion

Get examples of different book layouts in your CREATOR Library.

TAKE ACTION 3.1

What do your favorite books look like?

How do the text and illustrations flow together?

The Cover:

Front

Back

Spine

Interior/Front Matter:

   Half-Title page

   Title Page

   The Copyright

   Page Dedication

   Epigraph

   Table of Contents

   Foreword

   Preface

   Acknowledgments

   Introduction

   The First Page

Back Matter

   Bibliography

   Glossary

   About the Author/Illustrator

TAKE ACTION 3.2

Ingram Spark and Kindle Direct Publishing both have tools to help you gain clarity on your book size and what it could cost to print and distribute.[5]

What are your book dimensions?

Exterior:

Interior:

What is your word count?

How many pages is your book?

---

[5] https://www.ingramspark.com/resources/tools and
https://kdp.amazon.com/en_US/help/topic/GHKDSCW2KQ3K4UU4

KNOW THE DIFFERENCE

It's a common misconception that illustrators are responsible for designing and formatting children's books, and while these roles can overlap, each expert has a unique eye in the publishing process. The main focus of an illustrator is to visually capture the manuscript's tone, mood, and character development. A designer is typically hired before the illustrator and provides support throughout the process to create a cohesive layout for the book's interior and cover. They can offer their expertise in typography and color schemes that will appeal to your readers. Those hired after the illustrations are complete can drop the text in and ensure that the files are print-ready, though they will not offer much advice throughout the process. It's important to note that hiring for all these roles may not be necessary, but understanding their differences can help you assemble your dream team.

CONSIDER YOUR INVESTMENT EARLY

Investing in quality illustrations can make a big difference to the success of your book, especially if you plan on selling it. A dedicated illustrator will bring your story to life and make it more engaging for your readers. Alternatively, rushing or cutting costs can inadvertently limit access to your book and your message. While the cost of hiring an illustrator will vary based on your book's length, style, and the illustrator's experience, it's important to keep in mind that clip art or low-quality illustrations will not be enough to make your book stand out to attract and retain readers. You know what quality and dedication look like, and no matter what you spend on your illustrations, know that your mission, dedication, and love for your book will bring you the desired success.

Editor John Fox provides a helpful breakdown in his blog post on "How Much Does It Cost to Self-Publish a Children's Book?" [6] Based on hiring a U.S.-based illustrator for a thirty-two-page book, I've adapted his breakdown to the table chart on the following page.

[6] John Fox Bookfox, "How Much Does It Cost to Self-Publish a Children's Book?," Bookfox, August 19, 2023, https://thejohnfox.com/2022/05/how-much-does-it-cost-to-self-publish-a-childrens-book/.

COST	EXPECTATIONS	TIMEFRAME
UNDER $1000	Cut-and-paste style illustrations with limited customization and minimal detail. This category represents an entry-level illustrator, often located overseas.	Under 1 month
$2500 - $3500	Beautifully detailed and customized images that enhance storytelling. Involves a skilled illustrator, often with previous children's book projects under their belt.	2 - 3 months
$4500 - $5000	High-quality with intricate details and an intimate knowledge of book anatomy. Character and World Building.	4 - 6 months
$5000 - $12,000	Professionally crafted illustrations and typography. Though at the higher end, this category is reserved for illustrators who have experience in both traditional and independent publishing.	6+ months

Mindfully, these are estimated costs, and preparing yourself with a budget beforehand will prevent delays throughout your publishing journey. This is the time to remind yourself of who you are and what you set out to do with publishing your book. Take a break and organize what is important. Take account of your resources, network, skills, and abilities. Embrace the process with enthusiasm and an expansive mindset. Know that your book is now a vessel for expanding the lives of children and their families. It's no longer just about you; it's about the positive influence your book can have on young readers.

If you're working with a limited budget, you can hire an artistic friend or a family member to support you; your payment plan may be more flexible this way, or you may be considering illustrating your book. Leverage the vast wealth of resources in your community and online. Attend industry-led conferences and workshops, in-person or virtually. I regularly attend children's book conferences to stay current on the latest in publishing and marketing resources and outlets. In the meantime, I use Skillshare, a self-paced platform with a great community and instructors, to improve my skills and get feedback. If you use my custom URL, you'll get $50 off your Skillshare subscription and one free month.

Additionally, I offer regular coaching and accountability sessions for new and aspiring children's book creators to support you with real-time feedback, creative guidance, relevant experience, and thoughtful research throughout your journey. To learn more and book a Creative Coaching Session, visit BeeTheeART.com/lets-work-together.

HOW TO SPOT A SCAMMER

If you want original work for your children's book, take the time to conduct diligent research. Don't rush into decisions; verify and compare your options carefully. Review an illustrator's website, portfolio, and social sites to understand their previous work. A quick Google Image reverse search will help you determine what's original and what's been used before.

More recently, scam artists have gradually moved away from generic clip art images to generating higher-quality artificially intelligent (AI) images. While clip art is a lot easier to spot today with its dull looks and cookie-cutter poses, AI-generated art is becoming more sophisticated daily and more challenging to differentiate from what's drawn by an artist or generated by a programmer. AI can be useful for planning and drafting, even deciding on a style for the illustrations you want to see; however, it should not be used for finished production.

At the time of publication, you cannot copyright AI-generated works, and many self-publishing platforms are limiting the use of AI-generated art and stories.

A few things to help you determine if an image is AI-generated are:

- Check the hands and the eyes. AI images perpetually struggle with hands, focus, and human touch. (i.e., hugs, inability to look at a specific person or object, high fives, holding objects)

- Overly perfect and symmetrical or ridiculously improbable proportions. This may not be apparent initially but get a good look at the background.

- Unusual combinations or no distinction between the subject and the surrounding environment. Also, unusual repetition with no clear aim.

WHERE TO FIND A RELIABLE ILLUSTRATOR

There are various ways to find a reliable and quality illustrator, including recommendations from author friends, attending events, and searching within author/illustrator groups. Be specific if you post within a group; refrain from the infamous "I'm Looking for an Illustrator/Designer." That leads to hundreds of replies with little to no meaningful results. SCBWI is an excellent resource for hiring professional illustrators, although some are not in the market for illustrating self-published titles, so be mindful when looking through their profiles. Connect with multiple illustrators and ask for quotes or additional information before deciding. Check their availability and turnaround time to ensure they can meet your project's lifeline. Consider their experience and previous client feedback; this can give you an idea of their professionalism and work ethic. Stay optimistic and passionate about your book's potential. We'll peel back the layers into the process of How to Hire an Illustrator in Chapter 5, offering you valuable insights and tips to make this creative partnership successful. Keep going, and your dedication will shine through the pages of your children's book, leaving a lasting impact on young minds.

Vetted Illustrators

- Author Recommendations
- Your Social Networks, Groups and Timeline
- Recommendations from Friends and Family
- Society of Children's Book Writers and Illustrators (SCBWI) Illustrator Gallery
- Behance
- Upwork

START SMALL, THINK BIG

One of my favorite music groups, Michael Franti & Spearhead, has a song called "Start Small, Think Big." Earlier in my career, I discovered that even minor actions can move mountains. For example, if you come across an illustrator whose work you admire and want to collaborate with, ask if they have other options, even if their price is beyond your budget. You could begin with a consultation, inquire about their packaged deals, or see if they offer a price per image. Start with character sketches or commission a sample, which could generate pre-sale interest or even assist with crowdfunding efforts to promote your book. Choosing the right illustrator is an important decision that can impact the overall success of your project. Take the time to research and find a professional that you feel confident working with. Keep your eyes open; a great illustrator may be right under your roof or next door.

As an independent publisher, you have the power to shape the best possible outcome for your project. Chapter 6: Notes on Crowdfunding contains valuable tips from my experience and the statistics behind how to host a successful crowdfunding campaign, putting you in a position to get paid to launch.

Some authors even include the cost of hiring in their crowdfunding campaign. Author and "The Queen of Editing" Naomi V. provides an amazing example with her Kickstarter for *Why Am I Here? A Child's Book About Purpose.*[7] Illustrated by Megan D. Rizzo.

---

[7] Naomi V. Dunsen-White, "'Why Am I Here? A Child's Book about Purpose' - Kickstarter," Kickstarter, accessed December 20, 2023, https://www.kickstarter.com/projects/naomidunsenwhite/why-am-i-here-a-childs-book-about-purpose/description.

TAKE ACTION 3.3

Take stock of your publishing options, build your budget, and gather interview questions for potential hires. I have a list of questions to ask you during your interview in Chapter 5, but make sure you have committed to your final edit before hiring your illustrator to avoid drastic and costly changes. Here's a list of trusted illustrators in my network:

ILLUSTRATOR	WEBSITE	NOTES
BEE	beetheeart.com	
MARIAM POPPINS	www.mariampoppins.com	
TRAVIS THOMPSON	www.thesivartgallery.com	
ABIGAIL ROSCOE	www.coyote-studio.com	

WOLLY V.	@WollyV on Instagram	

NOTES

TAKE ACTION 3.4

Your budget lists can be divided into **pre-publishing, publishing,** and **marketing.** Some pre-publishing expenses include deciding on an editor or illustrator, while publishing expenses include printing and distribution costs. Marketing expenses can look like promotional materials, advertising, and book tours. Not all of these actions or materials will cost money; you don't need to tackle this right now. Take your time; I know you're up for the task.

PRE-PUBLISHING BUDGET

TASK	HIRED OR PURCHASED	NOTES	EXPENSES ALLOTTED	SPENT
WRITING SOFTWARE OR TOOLS			$	$
EDITOR OR PROOFREADER			$	$
ILLUSTRATOR OR GRAPHIC DESIGNER			$	$
COPYRIGHT (ESTABLISH AN LLC?)			$	$

ADDITIONAL NOTES OR REFLECTIONS:

PUBLISHING BUDGET

TASK	HIRED OR PURCHASED	NOTES	EXPENSES ALLOTTED	SPENT
PRINTING COSTS			$	$
ISBN REGISTRATION			$	$
ILLUSTRATION			$	$
COVER DESIGN			$	$
BOOK FORMATTING			$	$
DISTRIBUTION COSTS			$	$

MARKETING BUDGET

TASK	HIRED OR PURCHASED	NOTES	EXPENSES ALLOTTED	SPENT
BOOK LAUNCH PARTY			$	$
PROMOTIONAL MATERIALS (E.G. BOOKMARKS, POSTERS, FLYERS)			$	$
ADVERTISING (E.G. SOCIAL MEDIA ADS, PAID BOOK REVIEWS)			$	$
WEBSITE DEVELOPMENT & MAINTENANCE			$	$
BOOK SIGNINGS & EVENTS			$	$
BOOK TOURS & TRAVEL COSTS			$	$

You can find these ready-made templates and others in your CREATOR Library.

ADDITIONAL NOTES OR REFLECTIONS:

CHAPTER 4: NOTES ON BUILDING YOUR BRAND AND ONLINE PRESENCE

CULTIVATING COMMUNITY

One of the most common questions I see in indie-publishing spaces is, "When should I start marketing my book?" If you ask any pro, the short answer is "Yesterday." With the rise of the digital age, establishing and maintaining a quality social media presence will help support your book's longevity. Before we discuss "How to Hire Your Illustrator" in Chapter 5, I wanted to emphasize this because by building your brand and online presence, you can establish yourself as a credible author and create a community of loyal readers. Additionally, this can be helpful when hiring your dream team, as it allows you to communicate your vision clearly and effectively and provides your future team with some background information about you and your work. Your profile is meant to attract the people you want to work and collaborate with; it's not just a sales page; it should tell a story. Before publishing, you can share your ideas, inspiration, and progress on social media, generate buzz and excitement around your book, help build anticipation and keep you and your forthcoming book at the top of your audience's mind.

CURATING CONSISTENCY

A clear, informative, and engaging online profile tells your audience who you are, how you are helping others, and how to connect with you. This will be something that will grow as you do. Depending on your target audience and book topic, your personal profile may not cut it, especially if it contains mature content. As much as we would like to think we are in control of our profiles we can never be completely sure. It's important to remember that not only adults will see your content, and some potential readers may not be comfortable sharing pages with mature content with schools, libraries, media specialists, or museums. Consider creating a separate author page dedicated to your writing career to avoid potential issues.

This can help you better manage your content and attract more readers. A professional profile can build credibility, increase self-publishing success, and market your work more effectively. Social media is becoming more tailored to support businesses and creators by providing expanded tools to help you connect with audiences more likely to engage with your content.

Despite what many marketing gurus will tell you, curating consistency does not start and end with posting three times a day, every day on every platform. Marketing starts with a plan and is sustained by experience and strategy. Now that you're an author, marketing never ends. Yes, showing up daily is helpful and proven to increase engagement and sales, but how you show up is just as important. Plan how and where you want to show up, choose one platform, and maximize your audience where they're at; that way, you will not be burned out from working to figure out multiple posting styles and formats.

Make a few flyers to reintroduce yourself, celebrate your publishing process, and tell people how to stay engaged with you throughout the process! You can make these in Canva; they have more than enough free tools, including mock-up designs, to support you in curating your author profile, and they have the ability for you to schedule posts ahead of time if you have a business profile. Planning and scheduling posts ahead of time will free up a lot of energy for you to focus on developing your book.

NOTES

TAKE ACTION 4.1

I have had the opportunity to share space and time with some remarkable children's book creators of all ages who have inspired and taught me throughout this journey. They all specialize in different areas of children's book creation and exemplify what it means to build intentional and engaging children's book communities. Take some time to be inspired and browse their profiles so you can amplify your book brand, which you've hopefully been developing since Chapter 1.

KIM C. LEE

Kim C. Lee is the author of *Meet Frankie Jordan*, *Grand Joy*, and *The Night Owl* series. Her journey as a children's book author began with a gift of love for her son. Kim finds purpose and joy in writing stories, showing children the value of their experiences, and helping others accomplish their creative goals. She continues to write to promote diversity in literature and ensure that all children know their perspectives and experiences are valued. Kim offers a host of author services and lessons. Learn more about author Kim C. Lee at: https://www.kimclee.com/

MIKE WRITES FOR KIDS™

Mike and Barabara Gammage are the dream team behind their debut title *Dreamlighters Go to Space*. Drawing inspiration from his roles as a dedicated youth running and soccer coach, Mike has discovered a deep passion for creating meaningful stories for children. *The Dreamlighters Go to Space* is an award-winning children's book and the first of early guides encouraging kids to be creative, resilient, and service-oriented. Under the Mike Writes for Kids imprint, he hopes readers gain valuable life principles as they explore their dreams through his books. Learn more about author Mike Gammage at: https://www.mikewritesforkids.com/

KAJARA NIA YAA NEBTHET™

Rekhit Kajara Nia Yaa Nebthet is Chicago-born and the author of many books, including *Ra Sekhi Kemetic Reiki Level 1 and 2*, *I am Mind Body and Spirit*, *Light as a Feather*, *Sekhmet Rising*, and *Healing Ritual Magic*. Rekhit Kajara is a Heal Thyself Ambassador of Wellness, Medicine Woman, Priestess, Community Activist, Afrikaan Holistic Health Consultant, Spiritual Warrior, Sacred Woman,

Educator, Mother, Tree hugger, and Nature lover who has dedicated her life to promoting health, wellness, and natural living to our community.

Learn more about author Kajara Nia Yaa Nebthet at: https://www.rasekhihealing.com/our-founder

NIA OBOTETTE

Nia Obotette is a Milwaukee, Wisconsin, resident and HBCU graduate of Tuskegee University. Over the years, Nia has organized and coordinated cycling and running meetups with local groups like Black Girls Run and Black Girls Do Bike. Mrs. Obotette is the award-winning author of *The Exploring All I Can Do Series*. This series addresses the gap in the representation of minorities in children's literature and highlights the need for sports, fitness, and adventure books to reflect the diversity of our society. Learn more at: www.niatheauthor.com

KP CARTER

Kathryn P. Carter, M.Ed., also known as KP Carter, The Literacy Whisperer, is the award-winning author of The Lizzie B. Hayes Series, and a lifelong educator, TEDx speaker, and consultant. Her Rockstar Reader Academy is designed to meet the literacy needs of children, parents, and school districts. She is available to speak about children's literacy development and tips for aspiring authors. Her goal is to elevate, energize, and encourage children to become rockstar readers. Her Rockstar Reader Academy is designed to meet the literacy needs of children, parents, and school districts. Learn more about KP Carter at: https://www.kpcarterwrites.com/kp-story

DEDRICK AND HAELEE MOONE

Dedrick Moone and Haelee Moone are a passionate and dynamic father-daughter duo. Dedrick, an author, international motivational speaker, and Toastmaster, embraces multiple roles with joy and responsibility. As a devoted husband and proud girl-dad, he finds fulfillment in his family while making a positive impact globally.

Haelee, at the age of 16, is a talented author known for her empowering works, including "The Rules of a Little Boss: A Book of Self-Love." and "The Rules of a Big Boss," Her impactful presence has graced television, print magazines, and diverse platforms, inspiring readers of all ages. Learn more about Dedrick and Haelee: https://dmoone78.allauthor.com/

IFE, MUJASI, AND NYAME FATIU

Ife Fatui is a co-founder of Watoto Development Center and Urban Youth Initiative Project. She has been teaching and developing children for 15 years, community organizing for 11 years, lecturing, performing poetry, and writing for over 6 years. She is committed to the development of Afrikan people, particularly women and children. She is the mother of two children's book authors, Mujasi and Nyame Fatiu the authors of *My Baba, The Dinosaurs, and Me*, and *Why I Love My Mama*. Nayame and Mujasi are both public speakers, aspiring engineers, and scientists. You can learn more about Ife, Mujasi, and Nyame at https://ipetisutbooks.com/nyame-mujasi/

TAKE ACTION 4.2

Look over your social profiles, contact information, and website. Does it reflect the author you are becoming? For example, if someone looked at your profile, would they know you were a children's book author? How do they book you for an interview? Do all of your links work? Would you share your current profile with a school or children's library? Take note of what needs adjustment below:

BUILDING YOUR AUTHOR WEBSITE

As a budding professional, yes, you do need an author website. Social media might be the first connection, but it shouldn't be the only stop and not the main attraction of your author brand. Your website or landing page should be the central hub for your brand. While social media platforms offer opportunities to engage with readers and build a community around your book, these spaces can be temporary and restrictive. Your website, on the other hand, is a stable space that you can control and rely on for the long term. Don't worry about maintaining a website right now; growing and engaging an email list will help you communicate directly and effectively to your book audience.

A great hosting platform for your website or landing page will have an email or text integration or routing capability. Remember "The Great Social Media Outage of '21"? This outage effectively disconnected Social Media data centers from the Internet globally. Social Media users uproariously attempted to flock to other platforms, disrupting sites and servers internationally. I was planning a post for an author's event where I was speaking, so when it all went down, I could still connect with my email list to remind them of the event! While writing this book, there have been at least two other brief social media outages, which drives home my point: you can't keep all your contacts on one platform, especially one you have no control over.

STAY CONNECTED WITH YOUR AUDIENCE

There is longevity in building and maintaining some level of subscriber-exclusive content. In addition to paid subscriptions, Instagram has a DM-based broadcast feature that utilizes the "one-to-many" messaging tool to share updates, polls, voice notes, and more with people who want to engage with your content and stay up to date with your offerings. For now, the feature is exclusively for creator platforms, but remember that this should still be used as a lead generator toward your website or book landing page. Newsletters like Mailchimp, Substack, Mailerlite, etc. are great ways of sharing. Many authors also do a "newsletter swap" where they can engage with each other's newsletter lists. A key thing to remember whenever you're participating in community exchanges of any kind is choosing to engage with content that you have a genuine interest in and are willing to engage in meaningful contributions towards.

Once you have a healthy audience of personal subscribers, continue to nurture those relationships, even more so than your social profile. Provide value for your inner circle with insider tips and tricks, special opportunities to work with you, and early access to new releases. This will give you leverage to invite more people into your inner circles. Again, this will take creativity, planning, and organization, but I have some tools at the end of this chapter to help you build and maintain an engaging email list.

> *It really boils down to this: that all life is interrelated. We are all caught in an inescapable network of mutuality, tied into a single garment of destiny. Whatever affects one destiny affects all indirectly.*
>
> -Martin Luther King Jr.

TAKE ACTION 4.3

A subscriber list is a powerful tool for reaching readers directly, sharing valuable information with interested people, and  cultivating a strong community when you launch! I challenge you to invite new people to your subscriber list every week! If you already have a subscriber list, start re-engaging them today! Check in and give them a few life updates. Nurture your relationships where they are, not just when you want to sell them something. Access your CREATOR Library for a list of 77+ book topics to keep your email list flowing and engaged.

ENGAGING YOUR CREATIVE COMMUNITY

There is a special book for every child, and every child deserves a full library! There is no monopoly on children's books; we all have so much to learn and share, so engage with other children's book creators as much as possible. A pivotal moment in my children's book career was my first speaking experience at the *2021 Write The Vision Conference* hosted by author Felicia Brookins. I was privileged to speak alongside some brilliant book creators and marketing and publishing professionals I am grateful to say I still have in my network. Their stories inspired me to develop a more holistic view of each step in the creation process.

Surround yourself with people who share the same passion. During the conference, I had the opportunity to share the stage with best-selling author Kimberly Davis Peters. I loved what she said to encourage authors who were having doubts about the publishing process:

"When you have doubts, your kid-lit community will always be there to boost your spirits and answer your questions."

As a member of way too many children's book publishing and marketing groups, critique groups, and communities, I've experienced firsthand the generosity of my fellow creators, and while many of the same questions surface daily, there's always someone ready to provide valuable insights and answers. I recommend exploring previous posts and threads before presenting a question to the larger group. Many reputable recommendations have likely been addressed, offering a wealth of information to set you toward successful and profitable publishing.

TAKE ACTION 4.4

Introduce yourself to another author or a group of authors. Be intentional with the connections you make; do your research and ask questions. Most groups advocate for giving more than you take. That means not using this space to sell your book solely; use this space for learning and sharing what you have learned. Take your time with this process and get to know others through their profile you can journal about your experiences.

CHAPTER 5:
NOTES ON HIRING AND WORKING WITH YOUR ILLUSTRATOR

The following chapter includes sickness and images that may be sensitive for some readers.

BEFORE YOUR INTERVIEW

You've invested a lot of effort in shaping your book's concept, and now it's time to communicate your creative vision with your potential hires. Ensure you can schedule a conversation with them via phone call or video conference. I strongly advise against hiring someone without the option of direct communication via phone or video conference. There are some exceptions if you are hiring overseas, or there may be a language barrier; in that case, I suggest just keeping your eyes open to approach this interaction thoughtfully and with an open mind.

Before entering the illustrator selection process, ensure your manuscript and book specifications are ready. Familiarize yourself with your budget and establish a reasonable timeline. Remember that crafting quality illustrations typically takes four to six months. When plotting milestones and deadlines for your project, exercise mindfulness. While the urge to acquire images swiftly may be tempting, hastiness could lead to errors, strain your rapport with the illustrator, and compromise the overall quality of the end product. Reconnect with the overarching goals of your book and immerse yourself in your characters once again. How do you envision them? Explore their distinct personality traits and cherished possessions. Drawing from your initial research, having visual references in hand will significantly aid in capturing the precise style you aim for.

TAKE ACTION 5.1

THE INTERVIEW

Take some time to brief yourself before your interviews. Keep a tab open with the artists' profile and/or website up for a quick reference to pinpoint the styles that particularly resonate with you. Have your notebook and *Creative Composition Guide* on hand to jot down significant details and pivotal choices during the discussion. Do they have a list of books they have completed with other authors? Approach the interview receptively, as seasoned illustrators often provide insightful suggestions to amplify your vision. Embracing their insights can offer you a competitive edge in publishing and marketing.

Prepare some questions ahead of time. Your initial research will answer many of your questions, but here are some additional questions to get you started and keep you focused during your interview.

- How long have you been illustrating children's books?
- Have you worked on a book or books similar to mine?

- What is your process and turnaround time for a manuscript at this length? (Know your book length)
- What is your process for revisions and feedback?
- Are you familiar with the publishing process for children's books, including formatting requirements and working with publishers?
- How will we communicate throughout the project? What methods do you use to share progress and receive feedback?
- Are you working on any other projects right now?
- How do you handle potential delays or unexpected issues that may come up during the illustration process?
- How do you price your illustrations?
- How much would you charge to illustrate a manuscript at this length?
- Do you have payment plan options?
- Are you open to participating in promotional activities for the book, such as interviews, book signings, or social media engagement?

- Do you have a contract that I can review? What rights would you retain as an illustrator? (Typically, an illustrator reserves the right to use the artwork created for various projects in their portfolio.)

- What are your terms surrounding merchandise and marketing material?

TAKE ACTION 5.2

REVIEWING THE CONTRACT

The following is not, nor is it a substitute for legal advice. Please consult with a legal professional before you enter an agreement with anyone. Make sure the contract aligns with your publishing and marketing goals. Your Author-Illustrator agreement will answer these fundamental questions:

- Who are the contracting parties? What are the deliverables?
- What is the timeline?
- What are the compensation terms?
- What are the rights and usage details?
- How many revisions and edits are allowed?
- What is the termination policy?
- What types of files will be delivered?
- What is the confidentiality and indemnification clause?

Familiarize yourself with some standard contract terms and agreements on the next page. Remember that these terms will vary depending on the illustrator you're working with. It is common practice for illustrators to charge an extra fee for licensing their artwork for use in marketing materials beyond book publishing, including but not limited to toys, journals, stickers, prints, and more. I've highlighted where these conditions may vary; this may include revisiting and updating your contract every two to four years, depending on the expansion of your book. Collaborating with your illustrator for marketing materials offers valuable advantages as illustrators can expertly size images to ensure clarity and provide optimal formats for each project.

Elevating your book brand through marketing materials is a sound strategy, and it's essential to value and respect your illustrator's contribution rather than undermining their efforts. This is not to say that you cannot create content in a similar style and fashion; ensure your contract covers your marketing goals. I've provided a sample contract below; this is non-exhaustive and will take you to consider your budget, timeline, and specific book needs.

SAMPLE AUTHOR-ILLUSTRATOR CONTRACT

Contracting parties

Author and Illustrator's Full name, Business name, and all relevant contact information.

Project Details:
Title of Book:
Description of Project: [Brief description of the book and the type of illustrations]

Scope of work (Deliverables)

The Illustrator agrees to create [Number of Illustrations] for the above-mentioned book.

Both parties shall discuss and agree upon the style and theme of the illustrations before commencement.

Compensation

The Author agrees to pay the Illustrator a:
- One-time fee -
- Up-front Fee - and/or - Royalty Rate of (Agreed Amount) for completing the illustrations.

Payment shall be made in [Number of Installments] installments as follows:

[Details of Payment Schedule and Deliverables]

A NOTE ON ROYALTIES:

Be thorough with your royalty breakdown, and detail how you will document and distribute funds to your illustrator.

I worked with one client on an upfront payment plus "ongoing royalties" in 2021. I haven't seen one additional cent from that contract. So save yourself the headache of bad business and litigation, be honest, and be thorough.

Rights and Usage

The Illustrator retains the right to display the illustrations in their portfolio and for self-promotion. The Author shall have exclusive rights to use the images in conjunction with the book, including but not limited to its publication, promotion, and distribution.

Revisions and Edits

The Author may request up to [Number of Revisions] revisions per illustration. Additional revisions beyond this limit may incur extra charges at a rate of [Rate] per (Time/Revision)

Timeline

Both parties agree to the following timeline for the completion of the illustrations:

- Initial sketches to be submitted by [Date]
- Color Images to be submitted by [Date]
- Final artwork to be delivered by [Date]

Leave room for unexpected life events, revisions, and edits.

Copyright and Ownership

Upon full payment, the Author shall have full ownership of the illustrations, including the right to modify, reproduce, and distribute them as necessary for the book.

Termination and Governing Law

Either party may terminate this Agreement in writing if the other party breaches its terms. In the event of termination, the Illustrator shall be compensated for work completed up to the termination date.

This Agreement shall be governed by and construed per the laws of (Respected Cities and States). Any disputes arising from this Agreement shall be subject to the exclusive jurisdiction of the courts of (Jurisdiction).

You can review my contract at:
https://beetheeart.com/beetheeart-contract

BEHIND THE SCENES: AN ILLUSTRATOR'S ROLE

On October 24th, 2020, the day after my 25th birthday, I finished illustrating *Little Warrior Woman: Just Like Mama*. That day, I got a splitting headache that only stood out because I'm not usually prone to headaches. I thought it was nothing that a little extra rest couldn't solve, but quickly, I noticed sensitivity in my right eye. Over the next few days, I could see heat and rest were not working, and I panicked as I slowly lost the ability to open my right eye and rapidly developed a rash that splayed across my forehead, which caused incessant tingling and a fierce itch. A quick once over by my Telehealth doctor, who, without hesitation, diagnosed me with:

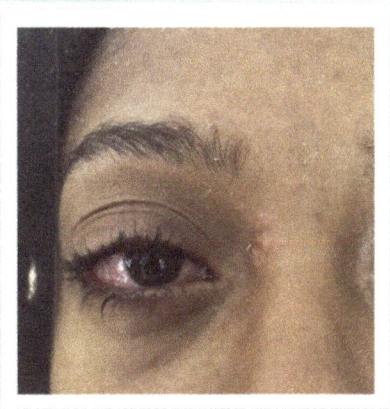

Herpes zoster, more commonly known as shingles, is a viral infection caused by the same virus as chickenpox, and in my case, it was ophthalmic.

Fortunately, the diagnosis came in time for me to receive treatment that prevented permanent damage to my sight. Although I still feel some of the sensations to this day, I was able to work through the challenges and deliver the final illustrations.

The next year, when *Little Warrior Woman* debuted, it freed up time for me to explore new ways to participate in the children's book creation process and generate multiple income streams if anything like that ever happened again. I attended my first children's book boot camp with *Storyteller Academy*. *Children's Book Mastery Bootcamp* is a week-long, fast-paced, free annual session hosted by Aree Chung and Myrna Foster. In addition to being introduced to the many levels of self-publishing and the business of being an author, I was also introduced to the bitter reality that more than a few illustrators had also suffered from Ophthalmic Shingles. My jaw dropped when I heard Aree mention this as one of the reasons why he chose to expand and supplement his illustration career. I had time to seriously consider the stress I was putting myself through daily, and while I genuinely wish I could wake up and draw all day, I have come to accept that that is not physically possible for me.

As an illustrator, producing quality and memorable work on any given day requires more than just drawing pictures. A non-exhaustive host of responsibilities can include:

- Manuscript study and consultations with the author.

- Conducting research and acquiring knowledge of the subject matter. For me, this may include traveling, visiting museums, virtual tours, and meeting with experts to co-reference material.

- Character design and world-building.

- Testing and determining the best color palettes.

- Storyboarding to avoid repetitive poses or scenery.

- While maintaining a sound, visual narrative with consistency and style.

- Thinking creatively to make illustrations engaging.

- Prinking knowledge and page layout to scale and export all relevant file types appropriately.

- Industry research to charge appropriately.

- Knowledge of trademark and licensing rights.
- Accurately predicting the time required to draft, revise, and complete a project to develop a realistic timeline.
- Repetitive rendering with excessive use of their eyes and hands.

In addition to these tasks, illustrators often go above and beyond to support authors throughout the publishing and marketing process. It's essential to recognize and compensate your creative team for their efforts. Even if you're doing this all yourself, knowing what to expect throughout your process and what you intend to pay yourself will be helpful when building your business.

Misunderstandings between authors and illustrators often revolve around price and time. There is a regular debate on what's "realistic" to pay for illustrations. How long should it take for illustrations to be complete? It's all relative, and it will take some time learning from your conversations with illustrators to decide what will work best for your timeline and overall budget. However, a pro in self-publishing will know that the most realistic price to pay their illustrator is what they ask for, and you get what you pay for.

As a dedicated author, you have taken the time to research and determine what you want your illustrations to look like. You have established a budget for your project and narrowed down a list of potential hires. You have clear judgment, and you know what your book needs. I frequently encourage my students to "do what works for you." It's a two-part reminder that while we all have our limitations, when it comes to accomplishing your dreams, sometimes you have to throw "realistic" out of the window and "do what works for you" because your dreams are too big to settle for less.

CONSIDER YOUR INVESTMENT LONG-TERM

Collaboration between authors and illustrators is often undervalued. Both businesses can greatly benefit when these two parties work together and support each other. After the release of your book, your illustrator can assist you with marketing by leveraging their network of followers who may be interested in the work you have created together. They can also help create marketing materials and assist with post-launch marketing efforts. By working together, you can expand your launch team and knowledge base, increasing your chances of achieving best-seller status. It's important to consider those who may miss out on something special if they don't see or read your book. Therefore, working with a professional, talented, and passionate illustrator can significantly impact your book's success.

In my collaboration with every author, I pride myself in seeing the success of our hard work come to fruition. I maintain regular communication throughout the illustration process, and upon completion, I provide supplementary materials like flyers, bookmarks, and promotional videos to help generate anticipation around their book. This support allows you to launch with confidence and the same enthusiasm you had when you began your children's book journey. Remember, creating a children's book is far more than crafting illustrations; it's a collaborative endeavor that shapes a timeless treasure destined to resonate across generations.

TAKE ACTION 5.3

If you haven't already, take some time to watch my segment during the Write the Vision Conference Hosted By Author Felicia Brookins on "How to Hire Your Illustrator," Where I review some of the topics we have discussed here and dive deeper into subjects introduced in earlier chapters, like where to search and what to consider when hiring the right illustrator for your children's book I also discuss more information on contracts, rights, and crowdfunding. You can view this in your CREATOR Library.

This knowledge is based on my personal experiences from 2019 - 2021 and is not exhaustive. However, much of the information remains relevant in 2024, not considering the cost of inflation.

CHAPTER 6: NOTES ON CROWDFUNDING

Crowdfunding is a great way to cover the cost of various stages of publishing and can be a helpful guideline to get you started on the right track to marketing with longevity. Crowdfunding is not limited to a few platforms; you can pre-sell from your website, reach out to donors, and write grants to fund your book!

"*$17.2 Billion is generated yearly through crowdfunding campaigns in North America, and it's estimated that number will increase to $300 Billion by 2030.*"

Maddie Shepard's blog "Crowdfunding Statistics: Market Size and Growth"[8] is a gem to gain insight into the numbers behind hosting a successful crowdfunding campaign and can help you decide if crowdfunding is a good option. While crowdfunding is often hosted on platforms like Kickstarter,

---

[8] Maddie Shepherd, "Crowdfunding Statistics: Market Size and Growth," Fundera, January 23, 2023, https://www.fundera.com/resources/crowdfunding-statistics.

Indigogo, and Fundrazr, applying the same techniques to fund your book with direct sales through your website is possible. Reading through this article was an encouraging discovery as my first two illustrated books were successfully backed and funded in different ways using many of these strategies. Gratefully, we had mentors and experts in our circle to support us in achieving our goals, AND had we known the numbers behind crowdfunding success, I know we would have had more systems in place to exceed our goal in the first few days instead of the last few - which I found out through reading this article, is also common! Stay focused and committed to your why and remind yourself and others consistently. Your *why* will be a top topic in every event and interview you speak at.

WHAT I'VE LEARNED FROM CROWDFUNDING

- Have a clear definition of your funding goals and an equally transparent budget. There is a community of people ready and eager to support you. Keeping an accurate record of your funding goals and accomplishments is a celebration for everyone in your circle! Refer back to your publishing budget and start with your basic costs. What's your number to break even? What's your number to profit?

- Prepare creative reward tiers and backer incentives. What are some supplemental materials that could support the launch of your book? This could be coloring or activity sheets, pencils, bookmarks, prints, journals, stickers, etc. Digital incentives are great because you can create many of these for free.

- Develop a comprehensive marketing strategy you and your team can commit to. Find the organization systems that work for you and schedule regular check-ins to review what's working, what can be worked on, and what needs to be dropped.

- Engage and invite people to your email list regularly. "Crowdfunding Statistics" reveal that 53% of email shares of crowdfunding campaigns convert to donations.

- Don't ghost your backers while you're working to attract newcomers. Your current backers can act like a megaphone for your campaign.

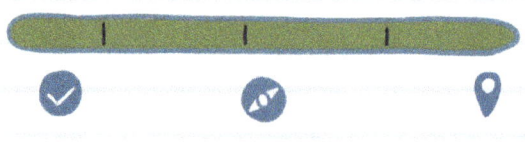

Shout them out and let them know they are valuable to your team.

CROWDFUNDING THROUGH KICKSTARTER: WHAT WORKED

A is for Alchemy: A Guide for The Little Conscious Creator was beautifully written by Esther Reese and initially funded through Kickstarter. In addition to Esther's diligent research and elegant way with words in both her literature and through her marketing and advertising, what worked well for the success of *A is for Alchemy's* Kickstarter is:

- Communicating a strong *why* and addressing a unique children's book needs.

- A proof copy on hand and ready to pitch worked well for us because it helped build much of the anticipation behind its official release.

- Connecting with people in our network to support our launch process got us into venues before we began our Kickstarter.

- Vibrant illustrations and key highlights.

- Enlisting professionals to support the creation of a book trailer and audio-book companion allowed us to provide an immersive experience for our new readers before they received their copy.

- Staying engaged and communicating with our audience regularly.
- It's more than just putting the book out there and hoping people will purchase it. You get out what you put in, and you, as the Author, can curate yourself to your bestseller success!

Writing the book is only half the battle; keeping yourself in front of your audience will require you to develop a clear plan. The amount of effort you put in directly correlates with the success of your book. You have the power to shape your image and ensure the success of your book.

Before the official launch of *A is for Alchemy*, Esther and I had already been talking about our dreams and plans beyond the book. I'm so grateful to my art family, who supported us early on our journey. My long-time mentor and networking virtuoso, Rubie Britt-Height, Director of Community Relations at The Mint Museum, booked us to feature *A Is for Alchemy* at their "Inaugural Neo Soul Café" in our then-shared hometown, Charlotte, NC. We had our first customer that day and a healthy email list eager and growing to support *A Is for Alchemy*. Wolly McNair is not only an incredibly talented comic-style artist but also a crowdfunding expert who supported us after the event to give us advice on how to host a successful crowdfunding campaign and provide an exclusive backer experience. This gave us the energy to push forward to deliver *A is for Alchemy* to many people who would resonate with it.

As any proud mother would the next day, my mom posted us on Facebook. The flood of support was astounding. Everyone wanted to know, "Where do we get this book?!"

Thank you, Mom, for putting us out there because, looking back, I don't think we would have moved so quickly on our own. That day, we began pitching to bookstores, experienced our first rejection, and gained a better understanding of pricing in the children's book market. We researched Kickstarter campaigns similar to ours and planned the best way to distribute them.

Esther and I worked tirelessly throughout the campaign to engage, promote, and connect with our community. Despite facing uncertainty and the possibility of not reaching our funding goal, we contacted bookstores, influencers, and fellow book creators in our network. It was Divine timing when @spiritualblackgirls responded to Esther's query and graciously shared our project. This resulted in an outpouring of support, and we were fully funded in the last three days of our project which, I found out in the article on crowdfunding, is very common. With the campaign's success, Esther took on more operational responsibilities, managing ads and sales funnels from Facebook to the book website, which took sales to the next level.

Crowdfunding and fulfillment can be a lot to tackle by yourself; in addition to generating sales for your book, you are responsible for managing your tiers to ensure your backers get what they are investing in. Esther recorded a beautiful, animated read-along video. I was grateful to be able to support them by creating supplemental material like posters, finalizing the coloring playbook, and taking on much of the initial fulfillment and distribution. Digital additions are great when launching a crowdfunding campaign because many of them can be created for free upfront and give your readers something to experience while they wait for their physical copies to be printed and delivered. Seeing how many families were excited that this book existed for their little ones was amazing.

Much of the profits and then some were re-invested to keep *A is for Alchemy* at the forefront of the hearts and minds of our audience. Since then, *A Is for Alchemy* has blossomed into an internationally known, loved, and debated treasure. You will face opposition from family, friends, and Facebook; remembering your book's message and the families that your book will help you stay focused on overcoming obstacles. Even when you face doubt, when people don't understand, standing firm in your *why* will consistently help you push past adversities.

CROWDFUNDING DIRECT

Crowdfunding through your website can be an exclusive way to release your new book before it becomes available. While it is mostly similar to platform hosting, the key difference is the all-or-nothing model vs. direct sales funding or keep-it-all campaigns. "Because of the lessened perceived risk, all-or-nothing campaigns are fully funded at twice the rate of the direct sales funding."[9] I didn't understand how these differences directly affected book sales and overall reach until I read the "Crowdfunding Statistic" article. However, it comes in knowing your audience, what they want, and how they want to receive it.

---

[9] Maddie Shepherd, "Crowdfunding Statistics: Market Size and Growth," Fundera, January 23, 2023, https://www.fundera.com/resources/crowdfunding-statistics.

My second illustrated title, *Little Warrior Woman: Just Like Mama*, written by Osunfemi Wanbi Njeri, was backed directly through her book website. Osunfemi already had a strong social media presence, but numbers aside, I watched her start where she was and expand outward. She began dropping hints and hosting LIVE talks and interviews with fellow creators in her network.

You can create a list of topics surrounding your book to discuss for thirty minutes to an hour if going live is something you think you'd like to do to leverage publicity for your book. Osunfemi did this consistently leading up to and following launch day. She used the website as a way to collect emails from people who were interested in purchasing the book. Those who subscribed to her email list received exclusive pricing the weekend before launch day, and anyone who purchased early received a signed copy and a private invitation to our pajama-themed launch party.

Consider continued crowdfunding through your website even after you reach your initial goal. This will keep the momentum flowing while you're gearing up for final publication and distribution. Start thinking about what kind of impact and community you'd like to build around your book. What memorable experiences can you share with your readers?

TAKE ACTION 6.1

We have been discussing the importance of pinpointing your *why*. If you're still unclear on what that may be, don't worry—we'll take some time to work through that now. It's normal for your *why* to change over time, but the truth of who you are and your book's message will carry.

There is power in understanding and articulating your why with clarity, consistency, and conviction. I think this is where many creators, myself included drop the ball, not because we don't know or don't care, but because when we're in the middle of walking in our purpose, we're not thinking about WHY we're doing it; We're just doing it! Call it spirit, intuition, or Divine purpose; whatever your calling is to what you are doing, trust that there is always something greater at work within you.

Take some time to meditate on that in your way. When you are ready, write down what comes to you.

When many of us think of meditation, we may visualize sitting still and quiet in a dark or candle-lit room, burning some incense, but meditation could look like taking a walk, listening to inspiring music, crocheting, or working out. Whatever puts your mind at ease for you to think clearly. You can capture your thoughts in your notes, hands-free with voice memos, or allow yourself to experience all that comes and note the important thoughts that stick afterward.

QUESTIONS TO UNCOVER YOUR WHY

What were you doing right before you decided to write your book?

What inspired you to sit down and write?

What were your favorite children's books growing up?

What connected you to those books?

Why do children and their families need to read your book?

What will they gain from reading your book?

How do you envision your books aiding a child's development and growth?

What legacy do you hope to lead and leave through your work in children's literature?

TAKE ACTION 6.2

Check out the *A is for Alchemy* Kickstarter and other successful campaigns by these inspirational children's book creators:

Why Am I Here?
Naomi V. Dunsen-White

Exploring All I Can Be Series
Nia Obotette

What Did We Miss?
Tiffany Semmons

Dreamlighters Go to Space
Mike "Writes For Kids" Gammage

CHAPTER 7: NOTES FOR UPLOAD AND PRINTING

KNOW YOUR DISTRIBUTION OPTIONS

Print-on-demand (POD) is a great and popular choice for new authors who are not ready to front the cost of bulk ordering. Print on Demand allows authors to upload, print, and ship their books at no cost upfront. With POD, the printing cost for each book will be higher, but it's much easier and less expensive to get started. If you opt for upfront printing, don't overlook your local options. Experimenting with pricing calculators, paper quality, and shipping requires time, but creating a book that children will love and want to hold on to is well worth it. Determining the final price for your book will be based on your preference for quality, return on investment, and how it compares to similar books in the market.

There are many self-publishing platforms; the most common combination authors use is Ingram Spark and Amazon Kindle Direct Publishing (KDP), so I will reference them frequently. In addition, you can reference *Fig.4, The Top Self-Publishing Platforms of 2023*, to help streamline your search and determine which platform is right for you.[10]

Ingram Spark isn't considered the most beginner-friendly platform, but I encourage you to take some time to learn the back office to take advantage of its extra benefits. Ingram Spark has significantly higher print quality than KDP and with the widest retail distribution, it makes it easier for independent publishers and bookstores to collaborate. While Kindle Direct Publishing has similar print quality, for now, they fall short in printing options overall and limit expanded distribution for non-Amazon retailers. At the time of publication, the royalty rates are lower on Ingram Spark than on KDP, but if you own your ISBNs, you can upload your book anywhere you'd like and determine which platform your book performs best. That's the freedom of an independent publisher.

---

[10] Yvonne Shiau, "The 17 Best Self-Publishing Companies of 2023," Reedsy, April 22, 2019, https://blog.reedsy.com/best-self-publishing-companies/.

TOP SELF-PUBLISHING PLATFORMS

PLATFORM	CONSIDERATIONS
AMAZON KDP AND ACX	Detailed educational resources. Wide reach and customer base. Limited Distribution. High-quality printing options. Limited hardcover options. Audiobook Production
INGRAM SPARK	Widest distribution range. High quality and a wide range of print options. Unreliable (Non-existent) customer services. Steep learning curve.
BARNES & NOBLE PRESS	Resources for authors. Cheaper printing costs. Limited Distribution.
DRAFT2DIGITAL	User friendly. Excellent rating in customer service. eBook distribution only. Done-for-you formatting.
KOBO	Canadian eBook distribution only.
APPLE BOOKS	Only available for Mac users. eBook distribution only. ePub formatting is required.
INDIE-AUTHOR PUBLISHING COMPANY IAPC	Wholesale Printing, Storage, and Fulfillment. Board Book Printing Options. Take a vested interest in the success of their Authors. Supportive Community.

LULU	Educational resources. A large author platform. Higher POD costs.
PRINT NINJA	Wholesale Printing. Now offers US-based printing. Great Kickstarter companion.
BOOK BABY	Easy to use interface. Weekly royalty payments. Board Book Printing Options. Higher POD and eBook setup costs.

KNOW YOUR PROGRAMS

Formatting and uploading your manuscript and illustrations is the most important process of creating your physical book. It can be challenging, and if you can budget to outsource this part, I recommend you do so. If you prefer to do it yourself, learn a formatting program and study your formatting guides. I spent countless hours on YouTube University and considerable investments in critique groups and creator platforms, and I'm still learning. But don't let that discourage you! It's possible to do it yourself with the right tools and knowledge. Some programs I recommend learning are:

- **Canva:** Canva has a limited use case but is great for designing your cover and a great platform for creating quick and engaging supplemental marketing materials.

Canva offers a free version and a paid subscription.

- **Affinity Publisher:** Affinity Publisher has a straightforward interface and is the next best thing to the Adobe Suite for a one-time fee.

- **Adobe:** Adobe is the industry standard for publishing children's books through Ingram Spark. Adobe is the only platform of the three that will export your files to a supported eBook format. Adobe offers monthly and yearly subscriptions.
    - Acrobat Pro
    - InDesign

Scrivener, Hemingway, and Atticus are also great for interior formatting tools as well as **Ingram Spark**. These platforms are better for text-heavy YA work, but I learned the hard way, that it's best practice to use **Microsoft Word** and build from there.

Most platforms will require an ePub file, which can be generated using formatting programs like Microsoft Word, Google Docs, or as a last resort, Pages.

COVER

For print books, many distribution platforms require you to upload your cover separately from your interior and provide a cover template generator for you to follow. Based on your book trim and page count, the spine will also be calculated and automatically generated within the document. Once the template is emailed to you, you'll need to arrange your document within the template and export it as a PDF.

INTERIOR

We discussed how to determine a trim size for your book, and if you hired a professional illustrator, they have already calculated the bleed in their initial illustrations, so now it's up to your design team to format your book and prepare it for print.

Bleed is important because it expands your illustrations past the trim line and prevents a white border from outlining every image.

BLEED

- Trim Height + 0.125 x 2 = Page Height with Bleed

- Trim Width + 0.125 = Page Width with Bleed

For example, if your trim size is 8.5 x 8.5, your file size for a single page is 8.25 x 8.125 and 8.25 x 16.25 for a full spread.

MARGINS

Margins ensure nothing important is cut off in the final trim of your book. You have margins on all sides of your document.

Margins with bleed should be set to at least 0.375 inches on all sides.

EBOOKS AND AUDIOBOOKS

Creating an e-book or an audiobook as part of your publishing and marketing strategy can be a convenient way to increase accessibility and sales. eBooks and audiobooks are cost-effective publishing options that can help you support various expenses throughout the publishing  and marketing process. Nowadays, readers preview, purchase, or check out a book electronically before deciding if they want a physical copy. Therefore, offering eBooks and audiobooks can increase your revenue and reader base. Audiobooks are also helpful for engaging younger audiences in learning how to read, providing a multi-sensory experience to your readers. If you are interested in producing an audiobook, Amazon Audiobook Creation Exchange (ACX) can connect you directly to audiobook producers who not only narrate your book but also provide "retail-ready audiobooks." [11]

Alternatively, you can hire an independent voice actor specializing in children's books, or if you're tech-savvy, you can record your audiobook in your in-home studio. However, producing a quality audiobook is not a quick process. It involves more than just recording yourself reading your book; it requires voice acting and creating an immersive experience for your listeners.

PREPARING YOUR BOOK FOR UPLOAD

Refer to your running list for your metadata. Based on your continued research, fine-tune your book description, author biography, keywords, and categories. Get clear on your pricing through market research, how much it will cost to print and distribute your book, and any remaining service fees. You want to cover the cost of production first.

---

[11] Amazon Audible Inc., "How It Works: A Step-by-Step Guide for Every Type of Creator," ACX, accessed December 20, 2023, https://www.acx.com/mp/how-it-works/authors.

Take some time to go back into your notes from **Chapter 1** when you found similar books, calculate the average cost of each, and continue to develop a budget sheet for your book launch and marketing plan.

Amazon KDP only offers pre-orders for e-books, but you can set a release date for your paperback. "When you schedule your book's release date, the Amazon detail page will remain hidden until your release date. While it's hidden, you can order author copies and promote it on your website or social media channels. Note that the book must complete our review process before author copies can be ordered."[12]

Ingram Spark (IS or Ingram) has pre-sale options for print and e-book formats. At the bottom of your setup page, you will see the options to set a **publication date** and the **on-sale** date; to avoid confusion, keep these dates the same.[13] You can set your release date to a year in advance, giving you more than enough time to order printed proofs and plan a successful book launch. To avoid misprints,

---

[12] Amazon.com, "Start Publishing with KDP - Amazon Kindle Direct Publishing," Start publishing with KDP, accessed December 20, 2023, https://kdp.amazon.com/en_US/help/topic/GHKDSCW2KO3K4UU4.

[13] Justine Bylo, "Setting a Sale Date for Your Book Marketing Strategy," IngramSpark, March 21, 2021, https://www.ingramspark.com/blog/on-sale-date-for-book-marketing.

early prints, or blank books, ensure you have all your files ready before uploading because once you select your distribution channels, if your book passes the review process, IS could print your book before your on-sale date. You can also order a proof copy to review before your book is available for sale. Make sure it's ordered far enough ahead of time so that you can make changes if needed.

SELF-STORAGE AND DISTRIBUTION

If you are ordering wholesale, you will need to plan for temporary space in your house or budget for a storage facility to store and pack orders to be shipped or held for upcoming signings and markets. A few things that would be helpful if you're planning on running distribution from your home-based publishing business:

- Invest in a thermal label printer and bulk shipping materials to preferably match your book colors and theme.
- Use this as an opportunity to market and pre-sell your book to cut down on your storage space and time. Have fun!

- Patron your local post office and ship media mail at least 3 weeks ahead of your estimated delivery date.

CHECK-IN WITH YOUR CREATIVE TEAM

Just because you can do it all doesn't mean you should. Despite its name, self-publishing can easily become a team effort, and there is no such thing as a one-person publishing house. Collaboration plays a significant role in the process; I encourage you to take the time to learn from and grow with your creative team and ask questions about their process. Their expertise is significant in ensuring your book is cohesive and consistent, keeping readers turning the pages, and their technical skills will set you apart in your marketing ventures, saving you time and energy to focus on what you love and help you generate more income. Even If you are taking Illustration, formatting, and publishing courses, get professional feedback and guidance.

Everyone on your team has a specialized eye for what they do and lived experiences to prevent you from making rookie mistakes. Embrace the process, learn what you can, and leverage the expertise of others to create a quality book that captivates your readers and helps you achieve your publishing goals.

TAKE ACTION 7.1

Review some Industry Tips and Tricks from Barnes & Noble Press' Formatting Guidelines, Ingram Spark's File Creation Guide, or Kindle Publishing Guidelines to help you better understand the formatting and upload requirements and determine how to engage your creative team and what you'd like to take care of yourself.

Barnes & Noble[14]

IngramSpark[15]

KDP[16]

---

[14] Barnes & Noble Press, "Book Formatting for Print-on-Demand," Barnes & Noble Press Blog, October 29, 2020, https://press.barnesandnoble.com/bnpress-blog/print-book-formatting/.

[15] Lightning Source LLC, "Self-Publishing Tools," IngramSpark, accessed December 20, 2023, https://www.ingramspark.com/resources/tools

[16] Amazon.com, "Start Publishing with KDP - Amazon Kindle Direct Publishing," Start publishing with KDP, accessed December 20, 2023, https://kdp.amazon.com/en_US/help/topic/GHKDSCW2KQ3K4UU4

TAKE ACTION 7.2

What distribution options are you considering? Take some time to explore the different platforms and ask your creative team what their recommendations may be. Is there anyone on your team who is already experienced in formatting?

TAKE ACTION 7.3

In Chapter 1, we focused primarily on our ideal reader, but your target market is the parents and loved ones who will purchase your book for their children. You are likely already in the same circles as your target market, but it's time to call them out almost by name.

- How old are they?
- What do they enjoy?
- Where are they hanging out online?
- Where are they hanging out in person?

CHAPTER 8: NOTES FOR DEVELOPING A STRONG LAUNCH PLAN

CLARIFY YOUR LAUNCH GOALS

Launching is one of the most exciting parts about publishing your book and chances are you will have multiple launches for your book. As you stand on the brink of publishing success, remember to set aside time, and reengage your plans and overall book goals. Planning will help you stay consistent and prevent burnout. This includes setting your launch date, detailing your strategies, and who you want to be a part of your official launch team. Late February through April (Tax Season) and June through September are popular times for book marketing and launches, gearing people up to buy for back-to-school, Black Friday, and all the winter gifting seasons. That doesn't necessarily mean your book needs to launch at those times, but it's important to study and consider market and consumer culture based on your book genre, topic, and target audience.

With the rise of crowdfunding platforms, 30-to-90-day launch windows have commonly served as the standard for independent publishers and marketers. However, traditional publishers capitalize on marketing their books **up to a year in advance.** During this preparation phase, traditional publishers cultivate relationships with advanced readers and reviewers; they orchestrate author visits and interviews, craft supplemental branded content, and review launch goals in collaboration with their marketing team. Pro publishers leave no stone unturned. One of my coaches, Darcy Pattison, wrote an amazing article, *How to Make Six Figures Publishing Children's Book*s, which completely shifted my approach as I work on publishing my own children's books.

One thing that stuck with me is her emphasis on the necessity to build a catalog of literary treasures if your goal is to generate substantial income by publishing children's books. This is true in traditional and independent publishing; series sell. Planning a series, will keep you at the forefront of buyers' minds and open up a host of opportunities to continuously engage with them in-person and online. Authorpreneurs Tiffany Obeng and Nia Obotette stand as prime examples of the forward-thinking and dedication it takes to build and maintain an extensive children's book catalog and thoughtfully planned series.

Thinking like a publisher means you're thinking ahead and planning your success.

Setting up a group meeting closer to launch day to discuss your goals will be beneficial in establishing guidelines for when and how to post reviews. Unfortunately, more authors have been caught **review-bombing** for their books and against their competitors. This is not what your launch team is for, and any unusually high activity will immediately flag your sales and review platforms and put your book at risk of being stripped from the market. You want to ensure the people advocating for you have read and enjoyed your book and are leaving honest, detailed reviews with photos when possible.

> Think like a PUBLISHER, not like an author.
>
> -Darcy Pattison

Your Advanced Reading Copy (ARC) is great for generating buzz around your book on Amazon, Goodreads, and social media, and it's customary for reviews to be posted up to two weeks before your launch date. Professional reviews are great for receiving unbiased, critical eyes on your work. Reedsy Discovery, Net Galley, Publishers Weekly, and Kirkus are reputable; however, paying for a review doesn't mean it will be good, and submitting for a free review does not always ensure someone will read your book. Booksprout and Bookfunnel are also good resources for indie-authors wanting reviews via ARCs.

If the review is positive, it will build a strong foundation for your new author career; if it's negative, it's a note for improvement, and no one has to see it but you. If you want professional reviews, plan at least two to four months to get a turnaround close to your launch day. Reviews are just one way to support your launch campaign. Remember, the key to a successful book launch is planning and organization. Stay focused, stay positive, and stay engaged with your audience.

CURATE YOUR CONTENT

Launching a book is not a one-day event. The time you spend clarifying your purpose and building your brand and online presence will serve as a supportive outline as you begin creating content for your book. If you have already tested some content, you can expand on what's been working and how to pivot where necessary.

We've discussed several ways you could launch your children's book. Ideally, you're at a place where you can use your characters in your marketing strategy as a fun and engaging perspective for your audience. Consider the time it will take to complete each task, the people you will need to hire, and the marketing material you will need to present to someone wanting to know more about your book.

Here's a brief overview of the launch strategies we've discussed and some additional ones you can implement in your book launch and marketing campaign if you want to create a fun and welcoming environment for your families on social media and offline. Each event will need to be broken down into smaller tasks and assets to support your launch and build excitement before and beyond your book's birthday!

- Host a crowdfunding campaign through a platform or your website.
- Offer supportive, fun, educational content, and resources to bundle with your book.
- Host your book-themed virtual launch event.
- Host, attend, and sponsor in-person events at your favorite venues, markets, and festivals.

- Plan a book tour leading up to and post-launch day, either virtually or in person.
- Run a social media campaign with your launch team.
- Prepare your author one-pager and press kit for your website so you can distribute it to book more author visits and interviews.
- Utilize high-quality flyers, videos, and thoughtful buyer-specific posts.
- Create a book trailer.
- Host a private group with your Launch Team.
- Run a special offering email campaign for your subscribers.
- Go live on your platform, by yourself, or with your team.
- Host a conference, webinar, or a multi-day experience.
- Create a book launch landing page.
- Write a press release and pitch to the news.

TAKE ACTION 8.1

Review your book goals and visualize what you would like your book launch to look like, who you would like to show up, and what you want to see come of it. Your book launch could be in person or online, but a best-selling children's book author does both. Take time to brain-dump some experiences you want to share with your audience.

BRAIN DUMP

BRAIN DUMP

BRAIN DUMP

TAKE ACTION 8.2

Organize your thoughts into strategies based on some main goals: Entertain, Educate, Engage, Support, or Interview. You can take this further by assigning a specific day to your launch activities. Organize in your own way. I'm sure you're familiar with the three reasons why we write, and you're probably wondering, when do I persuade? All of the time; you're always persuading your audience to spend their time, money, and attention with you, either passively or actively. For your supporting assets you want to think digital and physical: This includes flyers, email blasts, educational resources, tablecloths, stanchion signs, sign-up sheets, a landing page, professional photos, event links, and venue reservations. Be creative, inventive, and even a little outlandish. Don't limit yourself to what you feel like you can do on your own, enlist support from your team.

Launch Date:

Time:

Launch Team:

Location(s):

Launch Strategy(ies):

Start Date:

Until:

Supportive Assets:

- Educate
- Entertain
- Support
- Interview

Launch Date:

Time:

Launch Team:

Location(s):

Launch Strategy:

Start Date:

Until:

Supportive Assets:

- Educate
- Entertain
- Support
- Interview

CHAPTER 9: NOTES FOR MARKETING YOUR BOOK

BE SPECIFIC

By now, you have had some time to test and tailor your content and organize your launch strategies. It's time to refine your author brand, retain your true fans, and sell on an evergreen basis. Be highly specific in your marketing, connect with your community, stay visible, ask, and be prepared for the sale.

COMMUNITY CONNECTION

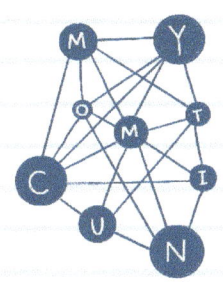

"Relationship-building is marketing." My first business coach, Jalynn Jones, consistently reminds us of this. Authenticity, intention, and impact are key to marketing success. Community connection includes holding space for potential buyers, peers, readers, and patrons; each relationship requires different attention. Maximize your relationships by inviting others into your community and investing in like-minded communities for advanced support. If you've never worked in sales, I suggest you take a course on sales and marketing; I know as an artist, I get very stuck in my world of creating, and I need a series of coaches to be able to market myself effectively. Get comfortable being a work in progress and have fun.

Where is your community? Where are the children who need your book? Are they at the library or the local after school? Are they at the baseball field or building LEGO? Are they in the foster-adopt system or children's hospital? Community is out there; you don't have to do this alone. Collaborate with other authors and influencers to host giveaways, panel discussions, and other literary events.

You can join our paid, private Facebook learning community of children's book creators to stay connected with the creators you've read about, ask us specific questions about publishing and marketing, share your wins, wisdom, and lessons from your children's book journey, and more:

VISIBILITY

Your visibility strategy will change depending on who you are working to connect with and during what time. Whether you're working on booking school visits, author interviews, or finally showing up at one of those book fairs or book-related events you wrote down in chapter one, you'll need to prepare for the pitch, the purchases, and the package or deliverables. That means preparing your author press kit, speaker contract, and purchase order (PO) forms.

The Pitch: in 2021, I focused on booking more school visits. I followed educators, school librarians, and media specialists in my area. I sent emails to subscribers to recommend me to school professionals in their network and sent 30 cold emails daily for a week. When pitching to schools, you want to research the demographic and curriculum, the school's yearly goals, and like interviewing for a job, you'll want to tailor your resume via your author press kit to show that the message of your book will align with their school vision and that your visit will be an asset for their students and families. Your press kit is valuable to send to news outlets, reviewers, and bloggers before launching and in your first few months. You want your one-pager ready to present at any networking occasion and ready to send when pitching your programs. Your author press kit should include your one-pager, educational material, and a prewritten press release. Your one-pager should highlight:

- Your name, relevant titles, and the best way to contact you.
- High-quality headshot of you and your books.
- Your mission, book, and description.
- Any relevant affiliations, awards, and sponsorships you have.
- Other relevant books and papers you have published.
- Your book brand, colors, and mood. Use your characters.

You can view and download my one-pager at:

https://beetheeart.com/about-bee

Review your speaker contract thoroughly. I can't stress this enough. We live in a tough climate, politically, and epidemiologically. It's becoming challenging to stay connected with children within the school system. Between the rise of book bans, political misinformation, and multiple threats to our national health, sharing diverse, relevant stories is our responsibility not just as independent publishers, but also as educators, parents, caregivers, and advocates for children.

In October 2022, I was invited to tour a school district in my state to share my experience as an illustrator. Between the district, my authors, and me, we spent a significant amount of time deciding which book to highlight, and The District ultimately decided *A is For Alchemy* would be "the perfect fit."

The following April, one day before the tour was scheduled to begin, due to an unfortunate decision by what we were informed to be "concerned school board members," the book tour was abruptly canceled due to *A is for Alchemy* being "too controversial." By the time the cancellation occurred, the district had been promoting our book event for months and had purchased over 7,300 copies. It was a clamorous wake-up call to some harsh realities of literary censorship in communities and schools.

There are tons of places you can share your book with families. You can host literary events at a local church, college, or museum. You can organize meetups at coffee shops and game stores. Consider pitching your local library or bookstore to host readings and educational programs. You'll need to donate a copy of your book to be cataloged in the library's system for library programs. When hosting events at bookstores, you must ensure the store can order your book through Lightning Source or Amazon. By trying out a few different experiences, you'll be able to stand out and find where you thrive in the marketing space.

The Purchases: We talked about offset printing earlier; some additional advantage to getting bulk copies of your book printed is that most schools and some bookstores will purchase books directly from you; you can order these at your author rate. You'll need to create a PO form to print, have it ready for your show or author visit, and email your purchasers directly. This will require you to forward their orders to your printer separately so you can get them at a lower rate to make a profit. Ordering bulk copies of your book will support your visibility and sales campaign. You'll always have a book to donate to A Little Free Library or a local bookstore, to leave in your dentist's office, or to forget at your next PTA meeting. With books on hand, you can submit physical copies to apply for book awards and reviews and to gift to influencers. It's time to put on your publisher's best.

A key visibility strategy that many self-published authors overlook is book award submissions. There are over thirty mainstream book awards specifically for self-published authors and illustrators, both free and paid. If you're a member of SCBWI, you can apply for the "Spark Award." Some other prominent indie-published book awards are *"The Purple Dragonfly" and* "The Royal Dragonfly" Awards from Story Monsters, LLC and the "Best Indie-Book Award." The Independent Book Publishers Association (IBPA) also has a Ben Franklin Award for all genres, including children's books. Winning a book award can greatly enhance your credibility and authority as a new author. However, not all book awards are worth applying for, as some are just flashy stickers from profit-seeking companies that pretend to be award-granting organizations. Fortunately, resources are available for authors to work together and identify scams and impersonators in the publishing industry. For an extensive list of reputable children's book awards, you can reference your CREATOR Library. I compiled this list from Friesenpress, The Writer Beware® Blog, and The Alliance of Independent

Authors which are all great places to stay aware of and avoid publishing scams.[17,18,19]

These lists are not exhaustive, but they have been established for at least a decade, and their winners have been vetted and selected by authors and illustrators worldwide. You can find book awards from various organizations such as arts and historical societies, councils and clubs, fraternities, and sororities.

SALES

Clear and direct, you want your book to make sales. So many new authors want to start with sales but need more information to support their sales goals. You can't just sell people cold noodles and call it spaghetti; you have to cut some stuff, boil some, mix some, and serve it in your best dish. How much money do you want to make in your first month? In your first year? Who are the clients you'll be selling to? In August 2023, I was awarded a

---

[17] https://www.friesenpress.com/self-published-book-awards
[18] https://selfpublishingadvice.org/about/
[19] https://writerbeware.blog/

business scholarship from our local community college to receive certification in government contracting.

For three months, I studied online and through 1:1 coaching with experts in business planning, organization, networking, and gaining access to capital. I had an amazing coach, Brenda Anderson, who sat down and guided me through charting my business goals and relationships. I organized those goals and mapped my services to cater to each level of my clientele for the next three years. It's still an evolving list, but for someone like me, who is bursting with ideas, it's immensely helpful for me to have a more holistic outlook on who I am serving to be able to differentiate my content based on where they are, and how I can meet and support them either through illustration, educational enrichment, or guidance through self-publishing. Some basic commerce terms that helped me to organize my sales strategies.

- B2C - Business to Consumer
- B2B - Business to Business
- B2G - Business to Government
- B2I - Business to Investors

What was also helpful was organizing what products and services could be scaled up, like digital real estate and merchandise, i.e., YouTube courses, and social media content limited to my physical time and energy, like 1:1 services and author visits.

TAKE ACTION 9.1

Set a goal number for what you'd like to earn from your book during launch week:

- Month One:

- Month Three:

- Month Six:

- Year Total:

TAKE ACTION 9.2

In addition to your book, what supportive products or services can you have in place to exceed those goals? List the prices and determine how many products or services you can sell to meet your goals. Your pricing will vary depending on who you are marketing your offerings to and how much it costs you to create and prepare for.

SUPPORTIVE PRODUCTS

PRODUCT/SERVICES	COST OF PRODUCTION	PRICING	RETURN	NOTES
HARDCOVER				
PAPERBACK				
EBOOK				

SUPPLEMENTAL MATERIAL				
AUTHOR VISIT				
CLASSES/ COURSES/ CONSULTATION				

TAKE ACTION 9.3

Who are some people, businesses, investors, and organizations you are interested in collaborating with? This wraps back around to the importance of relationship-building throughout your publishing journey. You never know who you will meet and who you will inspire along your journey.

REVIEWS

When you're having difficulty keeping the conversation going about yourself or need to break up some of the self-promotions, let the audience speak. In addition to the initial reviews you received from your launch team, ask your audience how they're enjoying their books and invite them and others to share their thoughts and experiences. Every time you vend at a show, do a presentation, share something from your book, or ask for a kind word or a reference for your book. Here are a few great ways to get reviews:

- Host a contest with your subscribers. If they purchase a book and leave a photo or video review, they can receive an "X" or enter a drawing for "X."

- If you've yet to publish, you can add a line to your description and back matter that encourages anyone who reads your book to leave a review.

- You can offer your eBook on Amazon for free or 0.99¢. I have seen this work tremendously for authors and backfire for others. The sweet spot offers it for a limited time, free every 30-45 days, to get reviews from people who may be interested. Remember what I said about diversifying your platforms and formats to maximize your opportunities as an independent publisher.

Stay away from the review for review trains unless you have exchanged books with an author or illustrator, and each of you can provide either a video or a photo review. Most of us invest in books that we hear others talk about, and the more we see others talking, the more we want in on the action. The more detailed your book review is, the less friction someone new will have in deciding whether to buy.

RETAINERS

Marketing should be a time to have fun and engage with your audience on different levels. Chapter 4 discussed building your author brand and online presence and not relying solely on social media to serve as your community container. We discussed building a subscriber list through your website and email. Still, now you want to think about how to maintain your community post-publishing and throughout your career. Publishing a series is highly recommended and can enable you and your team to work on similar projects with a consistent look and feel all at once (schedule and budget permitting). You've invested significant time, finances, and energy in establishing yourself as a children's book author; building upon the strategies you've learned throughout this guide will help you keep the fire burning. A retainer could be an apparel or accessory line, a regular membership or subscription, a paid course, conference, class, or training, in-person or online. There are a variety of author services and experiences you can offer. You are a community leader with skills, resources, and literary treasures to share.

TAKE ACTION 9.4

What marketing strategies have you tried so far that you enjoy? Why?

What are some less enjoyable strategies? Why?

How has your audience responded to your content? What are their responses giving you insight into?

How do you envision staying connected with your audience? What's your retainer?

Marketing is funny. We all enjoy buying the things we like, but very few of us enjoy being sold or marketed to. I encourage you to learn from what's being marketed to you. It can give you valuable insight into your marketing ventures. I won't get deep into marketing psychology, but I want you to be encouraged and aware when you face challenges getting or retaining engagement. When you're marketing fervently and purposefully, the right people will see and interact with you at the right time. You may not always get the likes, comments, shares, or views you intended, but know someone is watching. Give them every opportunity to see you "teach for the people in the back row." I hear Coach Jalynn whenever I THINK one of my marketing efforts is a flop or I do not see the reach I want. You never know who is watching you, bookmarking and saving their coins to work with you. It will take you to show up and give your best regardless of who is watching. Remember your *why* and keep your readers in mind; they deserve to see themselves in your book!

Marketing is an ongoing process; To keep you in your flow, I compiled nearly fifty ways to market and sell your book, which is available in your CREATOR Library. After reviewing your goals and trying some things for yourself, I recommend hiring an expert coach to show you how to market your book and services effectively. Hiring an author, or book coach (not solely a book marketer) who will help you learn the ropes, so you have the know-how to operate and delegate efficiently and responsibly, launch with impact, and sell on an evergreen basis. I've invested in a few coaches and courses, some fruitful and others fluff and confusion. I included a list of free and paid communities, classes, coaches, and additional author resources that I have attended or am currently a part of in the back of the book that have supported me in learning more about how to publish and market my children's book with planned success.

FINAL THOUGHTS

Congratulations again for taking the big leap and self-publishing a children's book! You just set yourself nine steps ahead in the publishing market! Your dedication will shine through everything you do. Other authors are ready to learn and be inspired by your journey.

You have navigated so many levels of children's book publishing and marketing. I am so happy for you and the children who will be inspired, uplifted, and seen through your book. I am happy for the families that will laugh, cry, share, and grow with your book for generations to come. I am excited to see you win, and most of all, I am grateful that you dedicated yourself to creating high-quality, relevant content for children to access. Thank you for choosing this guide to support you throughout your journey, but this is just the beginning. A preview, if you will.

My vision is for our children to be immortalized by incredible stories reflecting their beautiful, powerful, diverse experiences across time and space. This year will be dedicated to making that dream come true as I begin to navigate the publishing and marketing process for my own children's book, using my *Creative Composition Guide* to steer the course toward success. For you, that means If you liked this guide and want to see it step by step in action for you to follow along and reference, you can join me on my children's book CREATOR journey. This is your invitation to follow behind the scenes, beyond the page, and into real-life application in your CREATOR Library.

I am so excited to start this adventure with you, I look forward to seeing you there!

LET'S STAY CONNECTED

Website: BeeTheeART.com
X: @beethesage
Instagram: @beethesage
Facebook Group: Self-Publish & Market Your Children's Book - C.R.E.A.T.O.R Tribe

GLOSSARY

A

ARC: Advance Reader(ing) Copy - Copies of a book distributed to reviewers and influencers before the official publication date to generate early buzz.

ACX: Amazon Creator Exchange is designed to connect authors with professional voice narrators.

B

Bleed: Bleed expands your illustrations past the trim line and prevents a white border from outlining every image.

C

CMYK (Cyan, Magenta, Yellow, Key (black)): The color model used for printing; crucial for accurate reproduction of illustrations in print.

E

EPUB (Electronic Publication): A widely used open eBook standard compatible with various devices and platforms.

I

IBPA (Independent Book Publishers Association): a not-for-profit membership organization serving the independent publishing community through advocacy and education.

ISBN (International Standard Book Number): A unique identifier crucial for tracking and ordering your book. Make sure each format (print, eBook) has its own ISBN.

Imprint: An imprint or publishing imprint is a trade name, brand name, or subdivision of a larger publishing house.

K

KDP (Kindle Direct Publishing): Amazon's self-publishing platform for Kindle eBooks.

KWL (Kobo Writing Life): Kobo's self-publishing platform.

L

Launch Team: A group of people who have read and support your book. Your launch team helps build excitement around your book near its release date.

LCCN (Library of Congress Control Number): A unique identifier the Library of Congress assigns for cataloging.

LLC: Limited Liability Company

M

Margins: Margins ensure nothing important is cut off in the final trim of your book. You have margins on all sides of your document.

MG (Middle Grade): Denotes books for middle-grade readers, typically aged 8 to 12.

MOBI: Mobi file is a format for eBooks primarily used by Amazon Kindle.

Mock-up: A mock-up is an artistic rendering to demonstrate your book in action.

P

PB (Picture Book): A type of children's book primarily designed for younger readers, often with a combination of text and illustrations.

PDF (Portable Document Format): Commonly used for digital proofs and certain eBook formats.

PO (Purchase Order): A Purchase Order is great for ordering books in bulk for a school visit or trade show, it is a form your buyers fill out for you to submit bulk orders for your book.

POD (Print on Demand): A publishing model where books are printed as ordered, reducing the need for large upfront print runs.

R

Review-Bomb: When a large number of people or a few people with multiple accounts post baseless user reviews online to harm or inflate a person, product, or business.

RGB (Red, Green, Blue): The color model used for digital screens, important for creating digital illustrations or covers for eBooks.

ROI (Return on Investment): In the context of publishing, this measures the profitability of your book relative to the resources invested in its creation and promotion.

S

SCBWI (Society of Children's Book Writers and Illustrators): A valuable organization for networking with other professionals in the field, attending conferences, and accessing resources to enhance your craft.

SEO (Search Engine Optimization) Applying SEO principles to improve the discoverability of your book online.

T

Trim Size: The final dimensions of a printed book after it has been cut and bound.

Y

YA (Young Adult): Books aimed at teenage readers, usually aged 13 to 18. These books often deal with more mature themes and have teenage protagonists.

RESOURCES & FURTHER LEARNING

BeeTheeART.com/Creator-Library

Creative Pep Talk with Andy J. Pizza

Write. Publish. Sell. with Alexa Bigwarf

The Society of Children's Book Writers and Illustrators

Izzy B. Books

Children's Book Mystery with Karen Ferreira

Kindlepreneur with Dave Chesson

We Need Diverse Books

A Journal for Black Women Who Want to Write a Children's Book by Tiffany Obeng

Crystal Swain-Baits

Black Pretty and Paid University by Jaylnn Jones

The Barnes and Nobel Guide to Children's Books by Kaylee N. Davis

StoryTeller Academy with Aree Chung

Self-Publishing School Podcast with Chandler Bolt

Steal Like an Artist by Austin Kleon

The Artist's Way by Julia Cameron

How to Self-Publish a Children's Book by Eevi Jones

How to Self-Publish and Market a Children's Book by Karen Inglis

UNCLONED Marketing by Audria Richmond

BIBLIOGRAPHY

Amazon.com. "Start Publishing with KDP - Amazon Kindle Direct Publishing." Start publishing with KDP. Accessed December 20, 2023. https://kdp.amazon.com/en_US/help/topic/GHKDSCW2KQ3K4UU4.

Audible Inc., Amazon. "How It Works: A Step-by-Step Guide for Every Type of Creator." ACX. Accessed December 20, 2023. https://www.acx.com/mp/how-it-works/authors.

Bigwarfe, Alexa. "What Every Author Needs to Know about Copyright, ISBN, PCN, and LCCN - Write: PUBLISH: Sell. https://writepublishsell.com/, June 28, 2023. https://writepublishsell.com/isbn-lccn-copyright/.

Bookfox, John Fox. "How Much Does It Cost to Self-Publish a Children's Book?" Bookfox, August 19, 2023. https://thejohnfox.com/2022/05/how-much-does-it-cost-to-self-publish-a-childrens-book/.

"Bookshop.Org: Store Locator." bookshop.org. Accessed December 20, 2023. https://bookshop.org/pages/bookstores.

Brookins, Felicia, and Kimberly Davis Peters. "2021 Write the Vision Conference Hosted By Felicia Brookins," 2021.

Bylo, Justine. "Setting a Sale Date for Your Book Marketing Strategy." IngramSpark, March 21, 2021. https://www.ingramspark.com/blog/on-sale-date-for-book-marketing.

Dunsen-White, Naomi V. "'Why Am I Here? A Child's Book about Purpose' - Kickstarter." Kickstarter. Accessed December 20, 2023. https://www.kickstarter.com/projects/naomidunsenwhite/why-am-i-here-a-childs-book-about-purpose/description.

"Indie Bookstore Finder." Indie Bookstore Finder | IndieBound.org. Accessed December 20, 2023. https://www.indiebound.org/indie-store-finder.

Lightning Source. "Self-Publishing Tools." IngramSpark. Accessed December 20, 2023. https://www.ingramspark.com/resources/tools.

Pattison, Darcy, and Darcy Pattison Children's book author and indie publisher Darcy Pattison writes award-winning fiction and non-fiction books for children. Her works have received starred PW.

Friedman, Jane. "How to Make Six Figures Self-Publishing Children's Books." August 30, 2021. https://janefriedman.com/how-to-make-six-figures-self-publishing-childrens-books/.

Press, Barnes & Noble. "Book Formatting for Print-on-Demand." Barnes & Noble Press Blog, October 29, 2020. https://press.barnesandnoble.com/bnpress-blog/print-book-formatting/.

Press, Friesen. "Self-Published Book Awards." Friesen Press. Accessed December 21, 2023. https://www.friesenpress.com/self-published-book-awards.

"Self-Published Book Awards." FriesenPress. Accessed December 20, 2023. https://www.friesenpress.com/self-published-book-awards.

Shiau, Yvonne. "The 17 Best Self-Publishing Companies of 2023." Reedsy, April 22, 2019. https://blog.reedsy.com/best-self-publishing-companies/.

Vitale, Brooke. "A Template for Children's Book Layout, Pagination & Design." Brookevitale.com, November 2023. https://brookevitale.com/blog/childrens-book-layout#3-set-page-turns.

ABOUT THE AUTHOR

Bre'Anna Washington Weatherford, lovingly known as Bee, is a passionate author-illustrator and educator. She has served her community for nearly a decade and is committed to providing safe and nourishing spaces for young people to express themselves and confidently explore the world through creativity. Bre'Anna earned her B.A. in history, focusing on African studies, with a vision of providing our children with the wisdom, resources, and support to explore their natural talents, embrace their highest potential, and expand their cultural worldview.

Bre'Anna is the illustrator of *A is for Alchemy: A Guide for The Little Conscious Creator* (Esther Reese), *Little Warrior Woman: Just Like Mama* (Osunfemi Wanbi Njeri), *Cairo the Courageous* (Dr. Schenike Massie-Lambert) and *Spectrum of a Journey: A Guide for Caregivers of Loved Ones on the Autism Spectrum* (LaBeck Roe, MS)

www.ingramcontent.com/pod-product-compliance
Lightning Source LLC
Chambersburg PA
CBHW051620010526
44119CB00009B/223